Nancy Wilson possesses a sincere, deep, abiding faith in Christ and her faithful love [for] kids makes her one of America's true authorities in her field. If a little piece of her heart can reside in yours through reading Chosen With a Mission, *this will be one of the most significant experiences of your life.*
Dr. Joe White, president, Kanakuk Kamps, Inc.

So much has been written in recent months about the lack of direction for young people in our culture. Therefore, I heartily endorse Nancy Wilson's book Chosen With a Mission *as it offers a needed message of direction for young and old today. I look forward to giving it to many members of my parish.*
Rev. Edmund Griesedieck
Pastor, St. Alban Roe Catholic Church; Wildwood, Missouri

Chosen With a Mission *is a timely book for this generation and those who work with them. Many young people today are living like "kidnapped royalty." Nancy does a great job in letting the reader know that they were created for royalty, and the plan was established by God and will be fulfilled by Him when we recognize that we are gracefully His.*
Rene D. Rochester, director, Urban Youth Leaders @ Kids Across America, founder and president, Urban S.E.T.

Chosen With a Mission *is a powerful demonstration of God's work in the life of someone who has truly said, "Here I am. Send me." . . . Anyone reading this book will be challenged to go deeper and live a life of total abandonment to the Lord. Nancy Wilson has something to say that every young person in America should hear.*
Haman Cross
Pastor, Rosedale Park Baptist Church; Detroit, Michigan

Nancy is a true friend of our family. She loves the Savior, serves young people faithfully, and writes passionately. Chosen With a Mission *will challenge you to grow in your commitment to Christ and His work.*
Dennis Rainey, executive director, FamilyLife

Nancy Wilson is one of God's greatest secrets. Her life of faith is an adventure that is sure to challenge any Christian and to spur others on, who have picnicked too long in casual Christianity.
Jacob Aranza, author and youth communicator, Aranza Outreach

Nancy Wilson writes the story of how God can change lives in a personal and passionate way! If any woman wondered if living the Christian life was boring, Nancy proves no! If any woman wondered if serving Jesus was worth it, Nancy says yes!
Barbara Feil
Minister of women, Sunset Presbyterian Church; Portland, Oregon

Nancy Wilson has put into words her infectious enthusiasm and faith that have inspired countless numbers of teenagers and adults in her 25 years of ministry. Chosen With a Mission *is a timeless book that will bring you close to the heart of God.*
Chuck Klein, national director, Student Venture

[Nancy Wilson] walks with God and it shows. Here's a book that not only tells how you can walk with God too, but it shows you through rich examples from her life.
Paul Fleischmann
Executive director, National Network of Youth Ministries

CHOSEN
WITH A MISSION

Are You Ready for the Adventure?

Nancy M. Wilson

Chosen With a Mission: Are You Ready for the Adventure?
by Nancy M. Wilson

Edited by Erik Segalini
Cover and interior design by Sally Brown

Unless otherwise indicated, Scripture quotations are from the *New American Standard,* © 1960, 1962, 1963, 1968, 1971, 1972, 1973 by the Lockman Foundations. Published by A. J. Homan Company, Nashville, Tennessee.

Scripture quotations designated NIV taken from the Holy Bible, New International Version. Copyright © 1973, 1978, 1984, International Bible Society.

Scripture quotations designated LB are from the *The Living Bible,* © 1971 by Tyndale House Publishers, Wheaton, Illinois.

Scripture quotations designated NKJ are from the *New King James* version, © 1979, 1980, 1982, by Thomas Nelson, Inc., Nashville, Tennessee.

Scripture quotations designated KJV are from the *Authorized King James Version.*

Scripture quotations designated The Message are from *The Message,* © 1993, 1994, 1995, by Eugene H. Peterson. Published by NavPress, Colorado Springs, Colorado. Used by permission.

"The Mission" by Jon Mohr and Randall Dennis. Copyright © 1989 Sony/ATV Tunes LLC/Molto Bravo! Music. All rights administered by Sony/ATV Music Publishing, 8 Music Square West, Nashville, TN 37203. All Right Reserved. Used by Permission.

Library of Congress Catalog Card Number: 98-61308
First Printing, 1998.
Second Printing, 1999.
ISBN: 1-57902-010-0

Printed in the United States of America

Chosen With a Mission

Dedicated to My King

My heart overflows with a good theme;
I address my verses to the King;
My tongue is the pen of a ready writer.
Psalm 45:1

For who in the skies is comparable to the Lord?
Who among the sons of the mighty is like the Lord,
A God greatly feared in the council of the holy ones,
And awesome above all those who are around Him?
Psalm 89:6,7

Sing out His praises! Bless His name.
Each day tell someone that He saves!
Publish His glorious acts throughout the earth.
Tell everyone about the amazing things He does.
Psalm 96:2,3 (LB)

I dedicate these written words to my wonderful Lord, who has indeed captured my heart. They are offered to Him in humble gratitude for choosing me to be His, with the incredible privilege of walking in partnership with Him to fulfill His mission.

Introduction

A Call to This Generation

Would I win? Would they call my name? Surrounded by friends and co-workers asking themselves the same question, I stood in the office of our company's in-house travel agency, waiting, anticipating. Honestly, I didn't believe I would win the drawing for two free plane tickets, but I was all caught up in the possibility.

Then they called my name—my name!—and handed me two free plane tickets. Immediately, I began to dream about the city, the sites and the friend I could invite. But then my thoughts began to turn to my friends who hadn't won, and I began reasoning that maybe I should give the tickets away. *I do travel frequently,* I thought, feeling a little guilty. *Maybe I could give the tickets to my friends celebrating their 25th wedding anniversary.*

Reluctantly mulling this over in my heart and mind, I finally convinced myself that giving up the tickets was the best thing to do. Just a few days after winning, I returned to the travel agency to transfer the tickets into my friends' names. Again, I was surprised—but this time by the agent's response. "You cannot give these tickets away," she explained. "They have your name on them. No one else can use them. They are for you."

The feeling of excitement began to rekindle in my heart, and I wondered what adventure lay ahead for me. *This trip was exclusively designed for me*, I thought. *It was meant to be for me to go.* To this day, my dear friend Dawn and I share funny and exciting stories about the adventures we had exploring Seattle. We had the time of our lives making that memory.

Those tickets parallel the unique and special plan that God has for us. You have been chosen by God with a mission, one He created with you specifically in mind. He has a grand design for your life. And He chose you to share in this most intimate love relationship: to know Jesus Christ personally, and to walk in partnership with Him as He fulfills His mission through you.

As we journey together through these pages, dear reader, I'll tell you about my crazy life. I'll tell you about the summer I trained dolphins, or when I befriended a Satanist named Shadow Cat, or the day I spent locked up in prison. God used every wild experience to help me discover more about our wonderful Lord and how to walk with Him.

The road of life is also guaranteed to come with bumps, so I have written, too, about some of my own potholes and roadblocks, such as my struggles with an eating disorder. God carried me through it all, and I invite you, as you join with me, to ask the Father about His purpose and plan for your life. Really, this book is not about me; it's about each one of us. It's about you. And so I pray that the Holy Spirit will be your guide, opening your heart and mind to new insights about what it means to be chosen by Him. I pray these pages will prove to be an encouragement and a motivation.

God is pursuing passionate lovers of Himself among this generation. Together we can be united in the Father's love by fulfilling the specific mission for our own lives, as well as the mission He has given to our generation. Long before advertisers and the business world started talking about reaching out to the next generation, God had a plan and a destiny for us to fulfill, recorded in the Bible:

> That the generation to come might know, even the children yet to be born, that they may arise and tell them to their children, that they should put their confidence in God, and not forget the works of God, but keep His commandments (Psalm 78:6,7).

I invite you to pause here and pray along with me: "Father, open my heart, that I might fully comprehend what it means to be chosen by You for this dynamic partnership in fulfilling the mission and purpose You have ordained for me and my generation."

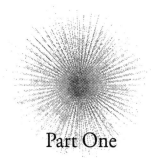

Part One

Chosen by Him

Long ago, even before He made the world, God chose us to be His very own, through what Christ would do for us; He decided then to make us holy in His eyes, without a single fault—we who stand before Him covered with His love. His unchanging plan has always been to adopt us into His own family by sending Jesus Christ to die for us. And He did this because He wanted to!

Ephesians 1:4,5; (LB)

chapter one

*But you are a chosen race, a royal priesthood,
a holy nation, a people for God's own possession, that
you may proclaim the excellencies of Him who has
called you out of darkness into His marvelous light.*

1 Peter 2:9

Royal Invitation

Big Ben, Parliament, the Royal Family—I was going to see it all. Thrilled by the possibilities, I hadn't wasted my overseas plane ride on sleep. Besides being my first international trip, this trip to England was an answer to my prayers and part of a desire dating back seven years. Now I was here, joined by a team of five other Christian youth workers, to help train and reach the high-school-aged youth of England. "Lord, make this a supernatural trip!" I had prayed as I boarded the plane. "Open up doors of opportunity that only You can, so that I'll see more of Your power. I want to know it's You working, not me!"

After the plane landed, our mission group grabbed our

luggage and drove together to the home of an English missionary. While everyone else tried to shake off jet lag, I decided to get up and go for a jog, figuring it was a great way to investigate the famous streets of London. Cautious about being in a new neighborhood, I used the quaint milk container out in front of the home as a mental landmark so I would recognize the house when I returned. How delightful to be jogging in the streets of London that October day! The flowers were beautiful, and the homes were straight out of a storybook, each one identical to the other.

Once I spent my energy, I decided to head back. That's when I discovered that *all* those storybook homes had milk containers out front, and in the exact same spot! The more I looked, the more lost I got. I didn't even know the last name of the people whom my group was staying with, much less the name of the street where they lived.

Two hours later, reminding myself all along to keep a sense of humor and enjoy the experience, I passed an older lady tending her flowers. "Hello! How are you?" I greeted her. "Your flowers are gorgeous!"

"Oh, darling, you're from America," she cooed back, noticing my accent. "Please come in and join me for a spot of tea."

Mrs. Vissar was delightful and charming, so much so that I almost forgot about being lost. Obviously wealthy and a lady of some importance, she spontaneously said, "You simply must be my guest at the House of Commons for tea!"

Suddenly aware of my sweatsuit and disheveled hair, I was feeling a bit self-conscious. "Me? Go to the House of Commons?"

"Yes, darling," she answered, "it's settled, two weeks from today!" She handed me a formal invitation, and we said goodbye.

Unbelievable! I thought, but then God reminded me of my prayer and I smiled in amazement. "Lord, You are full of surprises." However, my invitation to the House of Commons was only the beginning. I was still lost.

My confidence boosted by Mrs. Vissar's hospitality, I knocked at a door of another house, hoping the people inside might help me find my way home. This time I met a Jewish playwright who after hearing my story, gave me and my whole team complimentary tickets to his play at a London theater. First we engaged in a challenging discussion about Jesus Christ, and then he warmly directed me to the people on the block who also talked about Jesus. *What a great way to be known,* I thought. Thanks to God and my two new friends, I not only found my way back, but I bolstered my social calendar too.

Two weeks into the mission trip, my big day at the House of Commons arrived. As I got out of the bus and walked up to the impressive gates, I watched as others arrived in limousines and fancy clothes. The dressiest thing I had to wear was a simple jumper and a pair of Dr. Scholl's walking shoes. Believe me, I was no fashion plate, and at that moment I began to feel insignificant and embarrassed.

That is, until I presented my invitation to the handsome

guard in his tuxedo. He smiled at me politely, checked my name off his guest list, and then held out his arm to escort me inside. Suddenly I felt very significant. I had a royal invitation to an obviously royal occasion. (Mind you, I still didn't know exactly what I was attending.)

I was led to a lovely outdoor balcony overlooking the Thames River. Mrs. Vissar quickly spotted me and began introducing me to everyone, as if I were the special guest of honor. Waiters swarmed around each of us, pouring tea and serving exotic pastries and delicacies. Trying to savor every minute, I locked these memories in my mind.

"Ladies, ladies, the meeting will come to order," an older, sophisticated woman called out. All of a sudden these gracious, proper women changed their demeanor in a dramatic way and began to argue about "equal-rights issues." There I was, smack in the middle of an English Women's Liberation meeting.

Never have I experienced anything like it before. And just as I was getting over the shock, the leader interrupted the discussion to introduce a special guest. All eyes turned to me. "Please tell us," she said with great interest, "what the women of America think about this issue. Are they getting their rights over there?" Startled by the invitation, I stood up to address the lively group. This opportunity came rather abruptly, to say the least, but I gulped and offered a silent prayer to God for help.

"Obviously," I began, "there are struggles in America over this issue, as well as here. I suppose there always will be some degree of misunderstanding because of different views. However, one discovery I've made has really helped me to gain perspective on the problem."

These women obviously wanted to hear the American; they hung on every word I said. Thankful for their attention, I continued: "Roles of men and women don't seem quite as important as our true identity and worth as an individual. Several years ago, while in college, I came to understand a personal relationship with Jesus Christ. For the first time I experienced an unconditional love, not based on my position, status or sex, but based instead on my personhood. Jesus Christ set me free from stereotypical views of what I thought I 'should' or 'ought' to be. He allowed me the freedom to be who He created me to be."

At this point, I still had no idea what my audience was thinking. *Are they going to throw me out?* I wondered. But the women's group was still "all ears," so I brought my point home. "I honestly believe that the answer lies in Jesus' forgiveness of our own personal selfishness and our beginning to see ourselves and others from His perspective. This probably isn't what you expected to hear, but I think it gets at the root of the problem, rather than the outward symptoms. I'd love to talk personally with any of you after the meeting if you have any other questions."

Finished, I sat down and cautiously awaited their response. Miracle of miracles: They all clapped! Many women lined up to speak with me, hungry to know more about this spiritual relationship that I had described. Only God could have given me the words and the boldness to represent Him well in that situation.

"Oh, Lord," I prayed silently, "Thank you for the privilege of representing You! Who would have ever thought I'd be treated like royalty at the House of Commons?" I sensed His Spirit's gentle reply, *Why not, Nancy? You are a child of the King!*

What an awesome truth that I really belong to Him! God personally extended an invitation of royalty to me, as He does to each person born in this world. My experience at the House of Commons brought alive the reality of all I truly possess as His child. It helped me understand more clearly that I've actually been invited by Almighty God to partake of all His riches in Jesus Christ. His very life flows through me!

Like Mrs. Vissar out in front of her house, Jesus reached out to me when I was lost. He also gave me an invitation to royalty that I didn't deserve, and when I accepted it, I had no idea how important the invitation really was. But I'll know for sure on the day I approach heaven's gates and Jesus Christ welcomes me into His banquet hall of love for all eternity!

What about you? Have you accepted that invitation? Or maybe you don't yet know the secret to the treasure. Let me tell you what I found out back in my college days, when my boyfriend Wild Bill sent me on a treasure hunt.

chapter two

The Spirit and the bride say, "Come!" And let him who hears say, "Come!" Whoever is thirsty, let him come; and whoever wishes, let him take the free gift of the water of life.

Revelation 22:17 (NIV)

Secret to the Treasure

I love the song "Place in This World" by pop star Michael W. Smith. He reminds us all that deep down inside we each want to do something significant, to make a difference or leave our mark. When I was in high school, I wondered what the purpose of my life really was. I looked for significance in friends, popularity and achievement. Fulfillment seemed so temporary. Boyfriends came and went, cheerleading ended, parties grew old after a while. Oh, I managed to keep an optimistic attitude on the outside, but inside I was unsettled. Since a lot of my identity came from my performance and gaining approval from others, I found myself feeling like I had never quite done enough.

Voted "Friendliest Girl" in my high school three years in a row, I had tons of friends, managed to please my parents with good grades, and even went to the prom with the star football player. So who had time to deal with unanswered questions? Besides, I figured that everyone expected me to "have it all together," so I stuffed those doubts deep inside and went on trying to live life to the fullest.

I thought I could keep my feelings covered up, but psychologists tell us they come out, one way or another. When I was a junior in high school, mine came out through an eating disorder. Controlling food was a tangible way to control my life, so eating became a psychological obsession and a detriment to my health.

No one really knew about my eating disorder for a long time, only me and God. I had gone to church all my life and believed in God, but I was plagued with guilt, especially as my struggle with anorexia and bulimia persisted. I began to feel very unworthy of God's love. Still, I felt unable to stop the vicious cycle of overeating and then making myself sick. It was like I was enslaved to this habit. How could I be so out of control? It became easier to just live with it instead of trying to deal with it, especially since I had lots to look forward to in life, such as graduation and college.

College was exciting! I loved all the activities, new friends, and parties at Southwest Missouri State University. Never a dull moment—I took great delight in being where the action was.

Which explains why I liked Bill Lundergan so much. He was my college boyfriend, and everyone called him "Wild Bill." Knowing my appetite for adventure, he planned an all-out, wild-and-crazy treasure hunt for my 18th birthday. Wild Bill never did anything ordinary—one of the reasons I was attracted to him—and this was no exception.

A messenger arrived the morning of my birthday, delivering a tattered, old piece of paper. Burned around the edges, and looking ancient and mysterious, the paper invited me to embark on a treasure hunt. I was completely intrigued by the adventure ahead.

My first clue led me to a beautiful park where Bill and I had spent time together discussing our philosophies on life. (He was wild, but he could also be deep!) There, carved on a tree, was a heart with Bill's and my name in the middle. *How romantic and sweet,* I thought.

But to be honest, I felt a bit confused about my feelings for Bill. Though I enjoyed the security that a dating relationship seemed to bring, my feelings were so fickle that I got tired of each guy as soon as the newness wore off. I was beginning to feel that way with Bill, and now he was carving our names into history! I refused to think about it for the moment and decided to get on with my treasure hunt.

The second clue led me to our favorite restaurant, a popular hangout for all our friends. But in order to receive the next clue, I had to do something really bizarre in front of all my friends at the restaurant. What would they think? Popularity and acceptance were, as I said, important in my life. In fact, I made sure to surround myself with tons of friends and lots of parties. Yet there was always an underlying fear of what other people really thought of me. It would be nice to feel so accepted that it didn't matter what they thought. *Oh well,* I decided, *I might as well go for it!*

Singing to the waiter and kissing him wasn't all that bad. I did get a lot of attention!

Since I had to work for the clue, I figured Bill could have been more creative with the next destination—how ordinary, to send me to the college union. We were both involved in student government: He was the college union president and I was the travel chairman. But Bill knew how important accomplishments and grades were to me. He certainly helped to fill that need for significance by getting us involved in all sorts of activities, temporarily feeding my hungry sense of worth.

On with the treasure hunt. The final clue was a riddle that I had to decipher. It was very profound, going on about my search for purpose and meaning in life. More than any of the others, this clue really forced me to think. Somehow, my solution brought me to a sewer, a rather unlikely place to find my next clue. In fact, I figured I had made a mistake and was about to look somewhere else, when I noticed a ball of string on the ground with a note attached.

"You have been on a journey to discover the meaning of your life," the note read. "Look no more, the answer can be found at the end of the treasure hunt."

I could hardly imagine what was at the end of that string. As I pulled it up slowly, it felt light. *What could it be?* I wondered.

When I could see it, it looked like a poster. Slowly unrolling it, I did not notice Bill hiding behind a car parked close by. Yes, it was a poster, with a breathtaking sunset. But that wasn't all. There was a silhouette of a cross etched over the beautiful colors, and light beamed from behind the cross.

How amazing that Bill seemed to know that the deepest longing of my heart could only be found in the One who had destined my life to begin 18 years earlier. As Bill appeared from behind the car, all I could do was cry and thank him. I had reached the end of his treasure hunt, but this turned out to be just the beginning of my discovering the secret to life's treasure; that is, the Lord Jesus Himself.

During the first 18 years of my life, my search for security, acceptance and significance led me to many false clues. Though they produced a temporary satisfaction, they kept me from the real treasure. And following those clues opened up doors that caused pain and heartache. When Bill planned that treasure hunt, he didn't know that I had been praying, asking God to show me if there was more to knowing Him, if there was maybe something I had missed.

I had been raised in a religious home and therefore believed in a God who loved me. My problem was, I didn't think I could ever please Him enough or match up to His standard. I wasn't even sure I wanted to. I already worked hard to meet my own standards, plus doing what I thought would please my parents. Just thinking about meeting God's impossible standard left me feeling guilty and condemned.

Outwardly masquerading a perfect life with plenty of relationships, popularity and accomplishments, I was dying on the inside. Anorexia and bulimia became my secret way of coping with that internal struggle. But God was listening, and He heard my cries for help.

Shortly after Bill's treasure hunt, I was invited to a popcorn party on my dorm floor where the topic was "relationships." I was interested in the subject, but even more so because I knew the discussion would have something to do with God. My friends across the hall were hosting the party, and they were involved with Campus Crusade for Christ, an interdenominational Christian mission organization. Though my neighbors were much more subdued than I, their peaceful attitude and obvious contentment drew me in. What a contrast to my life of constant activity and outward excitement. People didn't know how restless and desperate I felt on the inside.

That evening I heard for the first time about God's unconditional love for me, a love that stands totally apart from anything I could ever do for Him. I learned about how much He desired a personal relationship with me. To think that God, Creator of the universe, also created me with a specific purpose and destiny! He came to give me life to the fullest—here on earth and eternally with Him in heaven (John 3:16; John 17:3; John 10:10).

Finally, I understood my dilemma. I was trying to live up to my own expectations and standards. But these standards developed because of my pride, thinking I could somehow be good enough for God on my own. That night my problem became crystal clear to me. I was separated from God because of my sin, my own self-will. And according to the Bible everyone faces this same problem. "For all have sinned and fall short of the glory of God" (Romans 3:23).

But God didn't leave me in this mess! He loved me so much that He sent His only Son, Jesus of Nazareth, who willingly died on a cross in my place, and paid the penalty for my sins (Romans 5:8). What security to have someone love me that much!

And that's not all. Jesus rose from the dead, conquering all control of sin, so that I could be forgiven and released from the effects of my sin. I understood for the first time why Jesus had to die, and I grasped the significance of His resurrection from the dead. I realized that if I could have made it to God on my own efforts, by living a good life, then Jesus didn't ever have to die. Jesus *did* have to die, and He did it just for me—each one of us—because no amount of effort on our part could ever attain God's standard of perfection.

This message was wonderful! I wanted so badly to be sure of my relationship with God. It was clear to me that He loved me too much to force me into a relationship with Him, but instead made it my choice: "As many as received Him, to them

He gave the right to become children of God, even to those who believe in His name" (John 1:12).

I wondered how I had missed the profound simplicity of His invitation in the past. The Bible further explains God's offer as a gift, something which is freely given. A light bulb went on in my mind when I heard the words of Ephesians 2:8,9: "For by grace [God's unmerited favor] you have been saved through faith; and that not of yourselves, it is the gift of God; not as a result of works, that no one should boast."

No longer did I have to try to earn this gift, but instead simply receive it with gratitude. The simplicity and beauty of God's love and grace caused me to question, *Can this really be?* After so many years of trying to be good enough for God, this news was like a cup of cool water to a tired, thirsty hiker struggling under a heavy backpack. In my heart, I knew it was true.

Like the verse in Ephesians explains, we've been saved, or rescued, from something. My friends explained that even if I could be good enough for God, I still wouldn't be able to pay my punishment for my sins. God Himself paid my punishment through Jesus.

> Then He saved us—not because we were good enough to be saved, but because of His kindness and pity—by washing away our sins and giving us the new joy of the indwelling Holy Spirit whom He poured out upon us

with wonderful fullness—and all because of what Jesus Christ our Savior did (Titus 3:5,6; LB).

Tears came to my eyes as I prayed a simple prayer that night to invite Jesus Christ to take control of my life. I knew I could trust Him, and Him alone. "Lord Jesus, I want to know you personally," I prayed. "Thank you for dying on the cross for my sins. I open the door of my life and receive You as my Savior and Lord. Thank You for forgiving my sins and giving me eternal life. Take control of my life. Make me the kind of person You created me to be."

March 15, 1971, marks the most important day of my life. I'll never forget how I felt when I realized that I never had to wonder again whether or not I would go to heaven. God was not weighing my good and bad deeds on His scales in heaven, but instead was seeing me through His Son, Jesus Christ, my Savior. Ever since that night, I have known and can say with confidence that I will spend eternity with Him.

He loves you just the same as me, and if you've never received His invitation to royalty, to become a child of God, it is my prayer that you would not read on until you open up your heart to Him. If you have any doubts about whether you have a relationship with God through Jesus, you can receive Christ right now by faith and begin the life for which He created you. You can end those doubts and know for sure, simply by expressing a prayer to God.

He knows your deepest thoughts and isn't as concerned with your words as He is with the attitude of your heart. I'd like to offer you a prayer similar to what I prayed when I invited Jesus Christ into my life. If you agree with this and it expresses your desire, why don't you make it your prayer?

Lord Jesus, I need You. Thank You for dying on the cross for my sins. I open the door of my life and receive You as my Savior and Lord. Thank You for forgiving my sins and giving me eternal life. Take control of my life. Make me the kind of person You created me to be.[1]

I feel a sense of urgency to plead with you—don't take God's grace for granted. Jesus loves you, He died for you, and God desires a relationship with you. I pray that today you will decide to give your life over to Jesus' control if you haven't already responded to His invitation. If you do receive Christ as your Savior and repent of your sin, you can be sure He will answer because of the trustworthiness of God Himself and His Word. You can also be confident of your eternal life!

And the witness is this, that God has given us eternal life, and this life is in His Son. He who has the Son has the life; he who does not have the Son of God does not have the life. These things I have written to you who believe in the name of the Son of God, in order that you may know that you have eternal life (1 John 5:11-13).

1 Excerpted from the booklet *Have You Ever Heard of the Four Spiritual Laws?* Copyright 1965, 1994 New Life Publications. Used with permission.

What an incredible promise for all eternity! As you put your life totally in His hands, you will begin the greatest adventure possible in life. The true secret to the treasure is that God has chosen us to be His, not to walk alone, but to walk with Jesus as our constant companion and guide. My adventure of walking with God started that night. I had no idea what lay ahead.

chapter three

*"For I know the plans that I have for you,"
declares the Lord, "plans for welfare and not for
calamity to give you a future and a hope."*

Jeremiah 29:11

Dolphins and
Double Backflips

"**H**ow would you like to train dolphins?" came the wild question.

"Me?!" I asked in shock.

"Well, you've taught kids to swim; why not dolphins?" Stan Perovich, my interviewer, replied. I was interviewing at Six Flags Over Mid-America in hopes of getting a fun job, but I laughed with delight at the thought of training dolphins. That exceeded even my wildest imagination! Sure enough, I did end up training dolphins as my college summer job.

That was my first summer as a new Christian, and only God knew the fears running through my mind. *If I really let Jesus run my life, it will be B-O-R-I-N-G*, I thought. *I thrive on*

excitement and adventure. I don't want a routine, predictable life.
Clearly, the Lord wanted to show me that life with Him in charge
would be even better than when I tried to orchestrate it alone. He
created me and really knows what makes me tick! In fact, His ideas
for us are way beyond what we could even imagine: "No eye has
seen, no ear has heard, no mind has conceived what God has
prepared for those who love Him" (1 Corinthians 2:9, NIV).

Actually, God had more in mind for me that summer than
simply keeping my life exciting. Through training these lovable
creatures, I grew in understanding more of God's ways. I guess
you could say He trained me as I trained the dolphins. For
starters, I felt an incredible need to depend on Him since I had
no experience speaking before large audiences. Yet with the title
of "Mistress of Maritime Merriment," I was suddenly doing six
shows every day to crowds of 2,000 tourists per show.

People would even come backstage because they wanted
to meet a live dolphin trainer. Of course, parts of the job were
not quite so glamorous, like having to cut up 13 pounds of fish
each day. But I loved swimming with the dolphins and listening
to their completely unique language, called sonar
communication. They are communicative mammals and also
very affectionate and relational. I learned how to communicate
with them through hand signals, rewards and a personal
relationship. In that short summer, I became attached to Buttons
and Beau, and they became attached to me.

As a young Christian, I saw a connection between this

experience as a dolphin trainer and my personal relationship with God. I learned that nothing could be more important than communicating with Him. My Heavenly Father wanted me to talk with Him and, through the Bible, I could listen to His answers. When I was swimming underwater with the dolphins, I heard their unique language and learned more about them than if I just observed from outside the tank. In the same way, I learned that summer about how to approach a holy God. Even though He welcomed me into His presence, He required a simple yet humble dependence on Him to provide for all of my needs.

And I got plenty of practice in relying on Him. One of the scariest challenges I faced that summer was to do my shows in a professional manner. I also wanted to be a witness for God to the people I worked with and the many people who came to see my show. That summer brimmed with adventures, not all of them smooth or easy. Like the time when I slid down the ladder and almost strangled myself on the microphone cord. Or the time when Spanky the sea lion began to bark violently at me, eventually cornering me in his cage. I had to pray for God to rescue me as I threw a bucket of fish in another corner for him to go after. (Spanky was cute, but who wants nearly 1,000 pounds of sea lion mad at you?!)

That was just the beginning of my adventure, walking with a creative and exciting God. He has become my dearest friend, confidant and partner in life's journey. He alone can guide us to the best path for our lives. And believe me, my life has been anything but boring.

But in spite of knowing that I had chosen the right path for my life, I still struggled with compromise at first. I wanted to hang on to my old way of doing things, so I tried to find out how much I could get away with while living my new life as a Christian. That was my motivation behind asking Marcie, my college Bible study leader, what I had to do to be a good Christian. She wisely answered, "Nancy, you concentrate on falling in love with Jesus, and He'll change your desires if you need to be changed."

It would be nice if I could tell you that I took Marcie's advice. But my compromises and confusion eventually resulted in my quitting the Bible study and all Campus Crusade for Christ activities. In fact, I went so far as to tell everyone to stay away from Campus Crusade for Christ—I thought they were a bunch of fanatics!

I felt miserable. My old nature of doing things without Jesus battled against my new identity in Christ as if a civil war were raging inside. This did not help my struggles with my eating disorder, either. All the internal stress caused me to slip back into old habits. Eventually I began to doubt whether or not Jesus really had come into my life. After all, how could He ever love someone as messed up as me? Yet, while this was all going on inside of me, everything looked picture perfect on the outside. I had learned how to hide all my insecurities and fears.

I'm so grateful to our merciful, compassionate Heavenly

Father. He saw me in my worst state and still loved and pursued me. All the while, He had Marcie and other friends praying for me consistently. Finally, I cried out to God, "Help me, Lord. I can't live the Christian life on my own. Show me what to do." He was waiting with open arms! But it was a process. Patiently God overcame my fears, reservations and rebellious heart time and time again, until He finally captured my allegiance. What a Prince!

Like my summer with the dolphins, Kanakuk Kamp stands out in my memory, marking another spiritual milestone. Besides fulfilling a dream to work as a camp counselor, the quality Christian camp provided a place for me to sort things out away from my friends and family. They didn't quite understand the changes that God was making in my life. That summer at camp drew me away from all the pressures of pleasing others, and I also met a bunch of Christian friends (not to mention some good-looking, athletic guys).

In fact, it was an attraction that began between me and one of the counselors that developed into life-threatening trouble. The trampoline instructor was seriously cute. During the work week, we were practicing on the trampoline and having fun. Johnny urged me to try a double back flip. With his great encouragement and my desire to impress him, I went for it. But in the air, I froze and came crashing down on my neck. I lay there in intense pain, unable to move at all, and tears came into my eyes. "Help me, God," I whispered desperately. For thirty seconds—and it felt like an eternity—I couldn't move. By God's grace, my whole body started to tingle and, less than a minute later, movement began to return my body.

They lifted me onto a stretcher and drove me to a local hospital. There, the doctor checked me out and advised immediate surgery. But the doctor's urgent recommendation frightened me, so I called my dad in St. Louis. True to form, he said, "Nancy, don't do anything with those doctors. You don't know how good they are. I will be right down to get you, and I'm going to take you to a specialist in St. Louis."

My dad filled the car with pillows and drove down at record speed to pick up his disabled daughter. Several people helped to lay me in my dad's backseat nest of pillows, and he then drove me to the specialist. To our amazement, the specialist contradicted the doctor at the hospital, telling me that I did not need any surgery at all. Time, he said, would be my healer. However, he did say that I had fractured my back. Had I fractured it one vertebra lower, I would have been paralyzed for life.

To this day, I feel a sense of amazement and gratitude to God for turning a complete disaster into an amazing example of His care for me. I returned to camp right away, but now no longer teaching tennis, swimming, water skiing or sailing. Instead, I taught nature and snakes (ugh!), but it gave me plenty of time to think. The events surrounding my trampoline accident painted such a picture of my Heavenly Father's care for me. Just as I had to come to the end of my resources, realizing that I could not do anything good for God, He was there, ready to come to my assistance. And as I watched Jesus restore my physical health after the accident, I began to understand that He had given me a completely new spiritual life as well. By reading the Bible, I saw that Jesus wanted to live His life through me. That's what this verse in Galatians means:

> I have been crucified with Christ; and it is no longer I who live, but Christ lives in me; and the life which I now live in the flesh I live by faith in the Son of God, who loved me, and delivered Himself up for me (Galatians 2:20).

By the end of the second summer, my white flag of spiritual surrender was flying high, and the battle was won. As the old song goes, "I have decided to follow Jesus, no turning back, no turning back. Though none go with me, still I will follow." And so sang my heart. I had been captured by the Lord once and for all.

As I began to experience the reality of Jesus living His life through me, He put a great desire in my heart to share that message with others. Being the first one in my family of eight and my circle of friends to talk about a personal relationship with Jesus Christ was not easy. In spite of all those awesome lessons God was teaching me, I sometimes felt alone and often felt misunderstood.

With my typically enthusiastic nature, I probably came on kind of strong to those people around me. (I've never been accused of being low-key). I remember one conversation when my mom started crying and my dad yelled, "Nancy, you're causing a lot of confusion! You've always been a Christian. It would be a lot simpler if you would just become a nun." I was totally "rocking the boat" in our religious home. Today we laugh about it, but back then it was painful. Nonetheless, God used that pain to draw me closer to Himself, for He was my Rock and my intimate Friend, the only One who always understood.

I also began talking openly about Jesus in my sorority and in the college union. I saw my priorities changing, but decided that if God was the one to change me, then I would let Him do it. That really became clear on the night when I went to one of my typical parties. My sorority attended a lot of parties on campus, but I distinctly remember the night when everything seemed different. Outside of God's work in my life, there were no explanations for such a marked change. But the alcohol tasted terrible, the smoke bothered me, and when my date began to put his arms around me, his forwardness turned my stomach.

God was indeed changing my desires from the inside out. I started going back to Campus Crusade again, and a speaker challenged me with this question, "Do you want to be a woman of faith?" I answered in my heart, "Yes!" The next part of the challenge was given: "Then go out and find the biggest tree, climb out to the end of the tree, jump and let God catch you." Wow! He continued with words that changed my life, saying, "Why don't you launch out in faith to do something that could only happen if God came through?"

A practical application of his challenge was to join a summer mission team for five weeks and tell people about Jesus in Mexico. The challenge resonated in my spirit. Yes, this was God calling me.

My parents, on the other hand, were not quite so excited. When I told my dad about the mission trip, explaining my confidence that God called me to go, he quickly responded, "Who am I to stand between you and God?" Even though my father paid for most of my college education, he reminded me that I needed to work during my summers to help him with some of my college expenses. How was I going to go on the trip and get a summer job?

"If God can accomplish that," Dad said, "then go." Underneath his skepticism and sense of humor was just the green light I needed. So I began to pray and ask God, "I want to go to Mexico, so what would be the plan, since I have to get a summer job?" As I prayed, the Lord spontaneously gave me the idea to find a church hosting a summer camp program. Since I was earning a recreation major and psychology minor in college, this seemed like a perfect match.

But I didn't know where to start. *God brought me this far*, I figured. *And it is His challenge. He will show me what to do.* I pulled out the local phone book and turned to the list of churches in the yellow pages. Then I closed my eyes, prayed, and pointed. Opening my eyes up, my finger rested on the name of Southwest Baptist church. I picked up the phone and called the number, explaining my situation.

The woman at the other end was amazed. "Please come down right now," she said. "We think you're an answer to our prayers."

"Well, you don't even know much about me," I answered.

"We have been praying," she replied, "and we just decided that if God did not find us a director for our camp in the next 15 minutes, we would have to cancel the camp."

Overwhelmed, I prayed as I drove to the church. I thought of God's promise in Matthew 7:7: "Ask, and it shall be given to you; seek, and you shall find; knock, and it shall be opened to you." What had seemed impossible to me was very possible to God. And sure enough, this Baptist church camp was the answer to my prayers. They hired me to plan their summer program, agreeing to release me for the mission trip, so long as I returned to wrap up the camp at the end of the summer.

But I still needed money to pay for the five-week mission trip. So I prayed again, and God gave me another idea. I decided to go around the neighborhood to all the people I had baby-sat for in the past. "I have invested in your children's lives for many years," I explained. "How would you like to invest in my future? I believe God is leading me to be a missionary someday. For a start, I'm going on my first mission trip this summer." To my delight, every neighbor gave generously. My trip was covered, and more importantly, my dad watched as my Heavenly Father faithfully carried out the call that He'd given me.

Since God's plans always proved to be unlike my plans, I should have expected more surprises on my mission trip, but I never imagined they would include getting typhoid fever. Shortly after arriving in Cuernavaca, Mexico, I, along with 90 percent of our group, came down with typhoid fever. Lying in my bed I felt rather useless to the mission, barely able to lift my hand, let alone preach the gospel. But in those times, it was as if God was saying, *All I want is you. You cannot do anything apart from Me. Make it your goal to know Me.*

I realized that I had nothing to give God except myself. Sick and in a strange bed in Mexico, I felt the warmth and love of God so strongly. I knew that only as I yielded my complete life to Him would I be able to really experience His purpose and presence. Being sick helped me to more fully grasp the words of the apostle Paul when he wrote,

> Yes, all the things I once thought were so important are gone from my life. Compared to the high privilege of knowing Christ Jesus as my Master, firsthand, everything I once thought I had going for me is insignificant . . . I've dumped it all in the trash so that I could embrace Christ and be embraced by Him. I didn't want some petty, inferior brand of righteousness that comes from keeping a list of rules when I could get the robust kind that comes from trusting Christ—*God's* righteousness (Philippians 3:7-10, The Message).

I did eventually recover from typhoid, and actually hiked into a remote village outside of Cuernavaca to share the gospel with the people there. My eyes were opened wide to the needs of people beyond my borders. I couldn't believe how open and hungry they were to know Jesus, but I knew then that I wanted to do this kind of thing more in the future.

That summer experience sealed my confidence in the power of prayer and in God's faithful plans for me. The Lord gave me confidence to believe Him for my family and friends who still did not know Him in a personal way. He promised me that He would work in their lives and eventually open their hearts to a greater understanding and hunger to know Jesus intimately. Eventually, my mother and father accepted the importance of my newfound faith and later, embraced a personal relationship with Jesus Christ for themselves. But that summer, they learned a difficult lesson about releasing their daughter to God and His plans for her life.

What about that college girl who told her friends to stay away from those fanatical Campus Crusade people? God called me to serve Him full-time with Student Venture, Campus Crusade for Christ's high-school outreach. God has a sense of humor and better yet, He has an individualized, perfect plan for each one of us.

Where are you in your journey? Are you still trying to live the Christian life on your own efforts? Are you resisting His will, thinking you need to hold onto your plans and dreams? I guarantee God's will is good, acceptable and perfectly designed for you. Let go and let Him lead you. Then step out in faith for the adventure of your life: "You have made known to me the path of life; You will fill me with joy in Your presence, with eternal pleasures at Your right hand" (Psalm 16:11, NIV).

Get a Hold of This!

Knowing you are chosen by God establishes a secure identity. Did you ever really think about what it means that God chose you? To *choose* means "to pick out, to select, to take one thing in preference to another." Remember how it felt to be picked for a sports team out on the playground? To be chosen is to be elected, esteemed, loved. These powerful words describe what God has done for us:

> Just as He chose us in Him before the foundation of the world, that we should be holy and blameless before Him. In love He predestined us to adoption as sons through Jesus Christ to Himself, according to the kind intention of His will, to the praise of the glory of His grace, which He freely bestowed on us in the Beloved (Ephesians 1:4-6).

God actually picked us out before the world began. He then adopted us into His family as His very own children with all the rights and privileges that go along with the family name.

Think of it! If we receive this free gift of salvation, this invitation to royalty, it is like we gain an inheritance from God (Ephesians 1:11). That assures us of His divine purpose for our life here on Earth and for all eternity.

We all have a need to belong, to feel needed and cherished in a special way. God put that need in us so He could fill it. Only He can meet the deepest needs of the human heart. Many of us discover that truth after trying to establish our identity on our own. In my life I tried using popularity, achievement and relationships, but they were deceptive substitutes. Instead, God wants us to respond to His love. He desires our trust and affection. We see God's heart for us as His children in the way He dealt with the nation of Israel, particularly in the following verses from Isaiah 43:

1) He created them, formed them and called them by name.

   "But now, thus says the Lord, your Creator, O Jacob, and He who formed you, O Israel, 'Do not fear, for I have redeemed you; I have called you by name; you are Mine!'" (v. 1).

2) He expresses deep affection for them.

   "Since you are precious in My sight, since you are honored and I love you, I will give other men in your place and other peoples in exchange for your life" (v. 4).

3) He chose them to be His witnesses.

   "'You are My witnesses,' declares the Lord, 'and My servant whom I have chosen, in order that you may know and believe

Me, and understand that I am He. Before Me there was no God formed, and there will be none after Me'" (v. 10).

4) He forgives and forgets their sins.

"I, even I, am the one who wipes out your transgressions for My own sake; and I will not remember your sins" (v. 25).

This is the mighty, merciful God we can know and serve! Just as God chose to reveal His glory through the nation of Israel, so He has chosen each one of His children to reflect Him in the world.

Have you established a secure identity in Jesus Christ? Are you growing in it? Ask the Lord to reveal any false securities you are relying upon to find your significance and worth. Confess them to Him, and ask Him to forgive you and help you to rely on your relationship with Him to meet the deepest needs in your life.

If you've never surrendered your life to Jesus Christ's control, that is the first step in the adventure He has planned for you. And if you know Him and love Him, there's no greater joy than allowing your life to be conformed to His purpose for you as you walk in partnership with Him.

A place to write your thoughts:

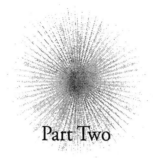

Part Two

Conformed to Him

And we know that God causes all things to work together for good to those who love God, to those who are called according to His purpose. For whom He foreknew He also predestined to become conformed to the image of His Son, that He might be the first-born among many brethren; and whom He predestined, these He also called; and whom He called, these He also justified; and whom He justified, these He also glorified.

Romans 8:28-30

chapter four

But grow in the grace and knowledge
of our Lord and Savior Jesus Christ.

2 Peter 3.18a

Grace-Fully His

Dear Jesus,

I know you are my best friend, and I love you with all my heart . . . why do I feel as if I can't please you? I feel so unworthy and guilty. I want to yield every area to you, Jesus, but I'm having a hard time on my own. Please do it for me, I'm too weak . . . Father, don't allow me to be content with second best. I want you to be totally in control of my life. Take every area, Lord, and let it be consecrated unto Thee!

—from my journal, December 5, 1973

I blew it again! Thoughts ran through my mind over and

over as I began to berate myself for my failure to discipline my eating habits. I imagined by now I would be over my horrendous struggle with an eating disorder. How devastating that I, who knew God's love and forgiveness, continued to harm my body and fall into this temptation again.

As a young college girl, I still struggled with bulimia and anorexia for several years after becoming a Christian. I agonized on my knees before the Lord, vowing over and over never to do it again. I cried out to the Lord, feeling disappointed, confused, and most of all, an overwhelming sense of shame. I had done so many other things right. I had joined a Bible study. I prayed. I even had a clothes sale so I could get rid of some of my outfits that seemed inappropriate for a young Christian woman to wear. So why was I still struggling with the sin of my eating disorder, even when I knew I was not honoring God?

I cannot begin to tell you how helpless I felt in this area! How often I failed after making promises to God. In my weakest state He revealed a liberating truth to me one night. I was going through some disappointment with my first Christian boyfriend, whom I had thought was perfect. He'd been knocked off his pedestal after letting me down, and I resorted to food as my consolation. After everyone in my sorority house had gone to bed, I snuck down to the kitchen and raided the cupboard. The momentary indulgence left me with a feeling of complete despair. *How could I do this again?* I thought. *After all, I'm a Christian— even the chaplain of the sorority! How could God forgive me again?*

I felt such total shame before God. All I could do was sob uncontrollably, and once again I begged Him to deliver me from this addiction to food.

God met with me that night through His Word. I still did not know the Bible very well, but His Spirit led me to the example of the apostle Paul's life. I identified with his struggle described in 2 Corinthians 12:8 where he pleaded with God three times to take away his thorn in the flesh. What a comforting thought that a leader like Paul might have felt similar to me. I didn't know what Paul's particular trial was, but I found great hope in God's response: "My grace is sufficient for you, for power is perfected in weakness" (2 Corinthians 12:9a). And Paul really embraced God's grace, as seen by his response: "Most gladly, therefore, I will rather boast about my weaknesses, that the power of Christ may dwell in me" (2 Corinthians 12:9b).

Now, granted, I could not completely identify with Paul. But the point I could identify with was the desire and prayer to have God remove my difficulty and my trial. It seemed that this addiction was something that went very deep. I felt as if the Lord were speaking to me, saying, "I am not going to just remove this miraculously. But My grace is sufficient, and My strength is made perfect in weakness."

Up until this point in my life, I thought that in order to be accepted by God, I had to have it all together. So much, I thought, depended on my performance. That night, the Holy Spirit revealed to me that I could embrace my weakness, that in fact, this would be the very way that God could show His power through a weak person like me. I was beginning to understand that grace played a continual role in my life, not only at the moment when I first became a Christian.

As I've thought back over the years of knowing the Lord, I can see the struggles I've had in understanding God's grace. The whole idea that God would give me something I don't deserve—in fact, cannot earn no matter how hard I try—is hard to grasp. But that is grace.

Through the eyes of grace, I began to see my struggle differently. My eating disorder became an opportunity for God's power to be shown in me. Since I felt so inadequate to overcome it, I knew it would have to be His power being perfected in my human weakness. What a hope! And did I ever need hope.

Needless to say, instant victory did not happen, but slowly, progressively, I learned how to rely on God's power when I was tempted and felt unable to resist on my own. I discovered ways of escape and alternative ways of coping besides relying on food. Ultimately, I began to accept and understand that only my Heavenly Father could fill my emptiness and pain. No person or thing could ever meet my deepest needs. Sometimes I'd still blow it, but the key for me was picking myself up again and not dwelling on my failure, but keeping my eyes on Jesus.

Some days I would just wake up feeling unworthy and condemned, even when I wasn't battling my eating disorder. I couldn't always trace it back to a definite reason, but when I could, it usually was some standard that I set up in my own mind and just wasn't meeting. I would cry out to God for help, forgiveness or acceptance, when in actuality He had already provided all those things for me, if only I could simply receive them. I would go back to Romans 8:1,2 over and over again, claiming this truth as my own: "There is therefore now no condemnation for those who are in Christ Jesus. For the law of the Spirit of life in Christ Jesus has set you free from the law of sin and of death."

A major key to conquering my eating disorder came from the help and accountability of some special people in my life. I discovered this at my first Christian retreat. Vicki seemed easy to talk to, and we had a lot in common. The Holy Spirit nudged me to share my struggle with her, but I was afraid. *What would she think of me after knowing that I had battled this terrible problem?* Though I didn't know the answer, I took a risk and confided in her anyway. I was so shocked when she admitted that she faced the same struggle. Only God could have directed me to a friend who could completely identify with this secret sin.

We began to pray for each other and hold each other accountable. It truly was the most important step in my healing. I understand now that whenever we keep something hidden, we can believe that we are the only ones in the whole world who have this terrible problem. That is absolutely not true. In fact, the Bible says:

No temptation has seized you except what is common to man. And God is faithful; He will not let you be tempted beyond what you can bear. But when you are tempted, He will also provide a way out so that you can stand up under it (1 Corinthians 10:13, NIV).

Understanding my need for more help, I also took a step of faith and revealed my struggle to two leaders working with Campus Crusade at my college. I decided to tell Marcie, who had led me to Christ, and her husband, Dwayne, and they counseled me through God's Word and particularly the book of Romans.

Meditating on God's truth and finding someone to hold you accountable in attitude and action, can be a very powerful safeguard against sin. By telling someone else about the temptations you battle, you pull the cover off your secret, and are no longer fighting alone. That's part of why God gave us each other! If you are serious about being Jesus' disciple, you will take precautions against sin as well as seek help if you need it. Jesus never condemns you for your weakness; rather, He waits to support and empower you to be a conqueror (Romans 8:37). Often, He uses His children to be that support.

Several years later, God sent me another very special friend to teach me more about who I was as a Christian. When I first met him, George Joslin was an 86-year-old man of exuberant faith and an ever-present joy in the Lord. Small in stature but bounding with energy, George obviously loved God and did not hesitate to tell anyone and everyone about Him. "What is Christianity all about?" my energetic, white-haired friend would boldly ask. Without waiting for an answer, he would quickly respond, "Jesus came to seek and to save the lost." George even made little cards about Jesus, and he gave them out to anyone he met.

I'd often ask George what he would tell young people if he were me. He looked intently at me and said, "Oh, honey, just tell them how great God is!" He had such an accurate view of God as well as a warm friendship with Him. Whenever we prayed together, I felt like I was in God's presence.

Like I said earlier, God used my friend George to help me understand my identity in Jesus. George often wrote me letters, and they usually began with great encouragement. "Hi there, God's Anointed!", he would write. Then he'd sign off with another reminder, such as, "I love you, little servant of the Most High God." But the message that rings the loudest in my memory is his constant emphasis of 1 Corinthians 6:19,20:

> Or do you not know that your body is a temple of the Holy Spirit who is in you, whom you have from God, and that you are not your own? For you have been bought with a price: therefore glorify God in your body.

"Do not let anything get you down," my friend would say. "Your body is the temple of the Holy Spirit within you! WOW! Jump up to smile!" He would constantly refer to the fact that it is Jesus living His life through us because He lived *in* us. It wasn't George's great faith that was the key; it was his faith in a great God.

Up until he was 90 years old, George worked with a prison ministry called the Bill Glass Evangelistic Association. He was instrumental in helping lead hundreds of prisoners to faith in Christ. And through teaching me by example about the way God saw me, George helped free me from my own prison—the prison of wrong thinking.

George died when he was 91, and I had the privilege of being at his funeral, a time I will always remember as his "home-going celebration." Often I ask the Lord to give my love to George, aware of the powerful impact he had in my life and the deep affection I still have for him. He was God's gift to me, and through George I was able to experience more of how the Lord felt about me.

How about you? Are you depending upon God rather than yourself to live the Christian life? As you daily rely upon His grace, strength and power, God will use you to lead others to Jesus and help them to grow in their faith. All God asks of us is to depend upon Him. I like to call it "being God's simple servant."

As I mentioned at the beginning of this chapter, I often felt inadequate and imperfect. The greatest revelation to me was that I *am* inadequate and imperfect, but that's OK! That's the beginning of the Christian life, recognizing my bankruptcy and His sufficiency. John the Baptist understood that truth when he prayed, "He must become greater and greater, and I must become less and less" (John 3:30, LB). I've made this my lifetime prayer: "Less of me, Jesus; more of You!"

Have you ever been in a situation where you felt in over your head? Have you ever asked yourself, what am I doing here—this job or commitment is beyond my capabilities? Take heart! Most of the men and women in the Bible felt that way. Take for instance, young Solomon, whom God chose to build the temple that David began. Even King David knew his son couldn't handle it on his own.

> Then King David said to the entire assembly, "My son Solomon, whom alone God has chosen, is still young and inexperienced and the work is great; for the temple is not for man, but for the Lord God" (1 Chronicles 29:1).

His father, David, prayed for his son earnestly,

> Give to my son Solomon a perfect heart to keep Thy commandments, Thy testimonies and Thy statutes, and to do them all, and to build the temple, for which I have made provision (1 Chronicles 29:19).

David's prayer was not for more ability, skill or talent. It was simply for Solomon to have "a perfect heart." What really counts is our heart before God, because once He has our heart,

He can fill us with more of Himself. Jesus Christ is all we need; He is our wisdom, our righteousness, our strength, our shield, our teacher, our leader, our mighty God. He is El Shaddai, our all-sufficient God!

Next time you are tempted, as I was, and feel "too simple" or "too inadequate," turn to Him for the reinforcement you need. God uses our inadequacies, fears and whatever other barriers we face to conform us to His image through a greater dependency. The joy of being a "simple servant" is found in being "grace-fully His." Just as you received Jesus by faith, so you walk in Him by faith. All by His grace, not our merits! Remember, dear servant of the Most High God, He must increase, and you must decrease. Enjoy the simplicity and freedom that is yours in Christ!

chapter five

Therefore having been justified by faith, we have peace with God through our Lord Jesus Christ.

Romans 5:1

Ticketed by God

Cruising down the freeway toward Springfield, Missouri, I suddenly noticed a flashing blue light in my rearview mirror. My stomach knotted up as I checked my speedometer—I was definitely speeding.

Immediately, I thought of my father. *Oh no! What will my dad say?*

I'd been out of college for 15 years. Now a staff member with Student Venture, I had just returned from my ministry's first pioneering mission project in Central Europe. I was on my way to show my slides from the trip to a church that had faithfully prayed and supported me on this missionary venture, so my dad had loaned me his new Buick. I had assured him I'd drive carefully, but here I was speeding. "Lord, Help!" I prayed in desperation. "I'm sorry! Please cause the policeman to have mercy on me."

But the officer, who was big and scary, did not smile at all. "May I see your license?" he asked sternly.

I handed my ID to him through my open car window and nervously began to make excuses: "You see, I'm just home from Central Europe, and I'm not used to my dad's big car."

"Ma'am," he coldly interrupted, "your license is expired."

Things were beginning to look worse and worse for me.

"Lady, follow me to the Lebanon station, where you can pay your fines."

By this time I started feeling angry. How insensitive and uncaring. Didn't this officer have any compassion or mercy for a poor missionary just home from Europe? It certainly didn't look that way.

As I followed him to the station, the Holy Spirit convicted me of my bad attitude. *You were guilty,* He reminded me, *and I do care about even the smallest areas of your life.* But I still struggled with my attitude so I prayed, "Lord, You are going to have to change my attitude fast, because I'm more angry than I am sorry."

The fine came to $110, but worst of all, I only had $25 in cash. What was I going to do? They would not accept a personal check, and they informed me that I couldn't leave until it was paid. It was now 7:00 p.m., and I was an hour and a half away from Springfield. My hostess was expecting me.

Tears welled up in my eyes, but I fought to keep from crying. The police officer walked away and left me with the jail warden. The warden directed me to a pay phone located inside a jail cell and told me to call VISA. They would have to wire money to the local truck stop so I could pay my fine and leave.

Clank! The warden shut the cell door behind me and locked it. Now I lost my composure and really started crying. Ironically, I had illegally smuggled Bibles on my recent European mission trip and had prayed regularly that God would protect us from getting caught. The Lord vindicated us over there, but now, back in the states, I was being locked up in jail. Now I felt like a criminal, and added to my shame was the truth that I had dishonored God by breaking the law.

I felt afraid and all alone. As I called the VISA office, tears flooded down my cheeks. Along with them, my contact lens rushed out. I was a mess.

"Ma'am," I blubbered into the receiver, "please don't hang up!"

Dropping to the floor of the jail cell, I groped around searching for my contact lens, my makeup streaming down my face. While on my knees, I prayed, "Lord, please forgive me and teach me whatever it is you want to teach me from this situation."

Romans 5 immediately came to my mind:

For while we were still helpless, at the right time Christ died for the ungodly. For one will hardly die for a righteous man; though perhaps for the good man someone would dare even to die. But God demonstrates His own love toward us, in that while we were yet sinners, Christ died for us. Much more then, having now been justified by His blood, we shall be saved from the wrath of God through Him. For if while we were enemies, we were reconciled to God through the death of His Son, much more, having been reconciled, we shall be saved by His life (Romans 5:6-10).

"Oh, Lord," I prayed, "this is exactly a picture of what you have done for me. Just as I'm guilty in this situation and without hope of paying the fine, with nothing but the law to accuse me, You stepped in. You knew that I could never make it to You through my own efforts. Even trying to be good and religious, I fall so short of Your holy perfection. When you suffered and died for me, You paid my eternal fine."

I've never experienced the reality of God's grace so clearly before. Touched by this fresh awareness of our Lord's great love and mercy, I cried all that much more.

When the warden finally returned to my cell, I asked to use the bathroom so I could fix my contact. He escorted me to the door. *Does he think I'm going to run away?* I wondered to myself. *Where would I go?*

While fixing my contact, the Lord reminded me that He had also died for the harsh policeman who gave me the ticket. I got my contact back in and my composure back together, and then asked the warden if I could talk with the officer.

When the officer returned, I apologized for violating the law and for crying so much. Then I told him how the Lord had deeply gripped my heart back in the cell, using my circumstance to show me the reality of what He had done for all of us. Curious, the policeman listened closely. Only God could have engineered that less-than-ideal opportunity.

When VISA delivered my money to the truck stop, two policemen escorted me to pick it up. I figured God scheduled this divine appointment as well, so from the back seat of their squad car, I talked with my guards about knowing Jesus personally. Like the first policeman, they listened with curiosity and interest, too.

At the truckstop, I got my wired money order, and I bought a big chocolate bar with my arresting officer in mind. The two guards took me back to me station to pay my fine, and after paying the speeding ticket, I presented the candy bar gift to the harsh man who first brought me to the station. I explained to him that this was a picture of God's grace, freely given. If I remember correctly, I think he even smiled.

Free to go, I went away amazed and thankful at how God turned this terrible situation around and used it for His glory. That experience will remain etched on my mind forever, bearing His loving signature.

It's funny for me to imagine myself behind bars, crawling

around on the prison floor sobbing, looking for my lost contact lens. On the other hand, I think of the accident God may have saved me from because of my negligent driving, and I'm humbled and grateful. But I think God got my attention to teach me a much bigger principle than just not to speed. He showed me how necessary it is for me to obey Him in every detail of my life.

If we are listening, He will speak to us throughout the day about each detail. I want to have an attitude like King David: "Search me, O God, and know my heart; Try me and know my anxious thoughts; And see if there be any hurtful way in me, And lead me in the everlasting way" (Psalm 139:23,24).

If we're listening to the Holy Spirit's prompting, we can confess our sin quickly and get back on course before it takes us further from God. Another way to describe that is "spiritual breathing," which is a phrase coined by Bill Bright, the founder and president of Campus Crusade for Christ. Spiritual breathing is just a simple exercise in faith that helps us to rely on the Holy Spirit's power to live the Christian life, and not our own power. Let me explain how it works.

Regular breathing has two parts to it: exhaling impure air and inhaling pure air. On a spiritual plane, we become aware of an impure attitude or area of our life that is displeasing to the Lord, so we need to "exhale," or, in other words, confess that sin to God. Confession means to agree with God that we have sinned and admit that we now want to change. By faith, we can claim Jesus' payment for our sin on the Cross and therefore receive

His forgiveness and cleansing: "If we confess our sins, He is faithful and righteous to forgive us our sins and to cleanse us from all unrighteousness" (1 John 1:9).

The second part of spiritual breathing is, obviously, to "inhale." This refers to a prayer of willing surrender to God's control. Through prayer, we can ask the Holy Spirit to run our lives and take over.

We don't have to be out of touch with God for one minute! Because He loves us, He doesn't want to have our fellowship and communication with Him severed. This truth has been the key for me in experiencing God's presence and direction moment by moment. The key to the process of spiritual breathing lies in surrendering that control to God on a consistent and regular basis. Just like it is important to "keep breathing" while doing aerobics or working out at the gym, you will stay in shape spiritually if you remember to keep spiritually breathing.

Have you ever been ticketed by God? Maybe you haven't been put behind bars by a policeman, but has the Holy Spirit ever arrested you? Has He ever grabbed your attention concerning an area of your life that was violating God's laws? He did it because He loved you, and because your sin would have likely ended up hurting you and others.

The Lord is "intimately acquainted" with all our ways, according to Psalm 139:3, and we're always in His watchful care. David asked, "Where can I go from Thy Spirit? Or where can I flee from Thy presence?" (Psalm 139:7).

At times we may want to hide from God because of our sin and disobedience. But if we are honest with ourselves, we know it only produces pain and separates us from the God who loves us and desires our attention. Our obedience to His commands helps us to grow in intimacy with Him.

What about you? Is there something you need to bring before God to confess and repent of, or change your attitude about? He is waiting to forgive, cleanse and fill you with His Holy Spirit. As we are conformed to His image, He shines His light on different areas in our lives so we can become more like Jesus. I urge you not to resist Him, but to respond to His loving voice. You may wish to pray the following prayer to God, or just pray one in your own words.

Dear Father, I need You. I admit that I have been in control of my life, and that, as a result, I have sinned against You. I thank You that You have forgiven my sins through Christ's death on the cross for me. I now invite Christ to again take control of my life. Fill me with the Holy Spirit as You command me to be filled. You promise in Your Word that You would do it if I asked in faith. I pray this in the name of Jesus. As an expression of my faith, I now thank You for taking control of my life and for filling me with the Holy Spirit.

It's important to understand that these are not magical words, guaranteed to fill you with the Holy Spirit. God releases His power to us through our faith in Him and in His Word, not because we put the right words together and say them with our mouths. Another thing to remember is that, just like you need to breathe in and out all day long, you may find yourself regularly needing to confess your sin to God and giving the control back over to Him. That's OK! Be honest with Him and confess as often as you need to. Unless we consciously have clean hearts before God, He cannot fill us with His Holy Spirit. And if we aren't surrendered to Him, we will be missing out on the daily adventure He has for us!

chapter six

Assemble the people to Me, that I may let them hear My words so they may learn to fear Me all the days they live on the earth, and that they may teach their children.

Deuteronomy 4:10

Freedom and Fear

"Lord," I prayed, "continue to conform me to Your image. Please remove any false securities or things that bring me significance apart from You." This was my heart's desire as I went into the summer of 1987. I was expecting God might answer my prayers through my challenging summer of study as I did research for my master's project. The project involved researching historical and biblical examples of God using young people throughout history. What I didn't expect was that God would shut down my voice box to answer my prayers.

Shortly after I arrived at Colorado State University, where I would be studying all summer, I went up to speak at the Rocky

Mountain Getaway, another of our Student Venture week-long conferences. The night before, while talking to the waiter about Jesus Christ, I lost my voice. It was that abrupt! One minute I could talk, the next I didn't have a voice.

This was the beginning of a long summer of no voice at all. I was told I had strained my vocal cords. Along with that came a severe cough and sores in my mouth. I prayed daily for God to heal me, and thanked Him by faith that He was in control. He blessed me with Shirley, a dear friend and roommate who helped explain to everyone what I wanted and why I couldn't talk.

At first not being able to speak wasn't so bad, but when it lingered on and on, it became a trial. The Lord used it to reveal more of His perspective to me. After praying one night and reading in the Bible, I turned to the book of Job. Within those pages, the Lord reminded me that His main purpose for me was not to accomplish some great thing, but simply to glorify Himself. Job, I read, was faithful to God, even in His darkest hour of suffering. My trial seemed so trivial in comparison, but I wanted to glorify God in it like Job did. According to 2 Corinthians, we all can: "But we have this treasure in earthen vessels, that the surpassing greatness of the power may be of God and not from ourselves" (4:7). "Lord," I prayed quietly (I certainly couldn't shout it), "glorify Yourself through my body, even though it's not working too well right now."

That summer, God continued to strip away some of my securities so I could see what was really important to Him.

During my trial of having no voice, God revealed to me how much I had based my identity and self-worth on my accomplishments or on the opinions of others. I understood a root issue that needed to change: namely, that I operated in life more from a fear of man than a fear of God. Author Joy Dawson explains this concept of "fearing man" in her book, *Intimate Friendship With God:* "The fear of man is being more impressed with man's reaction to our actions than with God's reaction. That's bondage."[1]

My vocal trial continued beyond that summer, lingering off and on for several years. God used my voice (or lack of it) as a training tool and to get my attention. At one point my doctor warned me that the problem risked becoming cancerous. In this dark valley of life, both physically and emotionally, the lesson which the Holy Spirit wanted to teach me was about the fear of the Lord. In contrast to Joy Dawson's definition of fearing man, she wrote this explanation of fearing God (in the same book): "When we have the fear of God upon us, we are impressed only with God's reaction. We are freed from the concern of what people think. That's freedom!"[2]

My trial without a voice forced me to see that God alone was my audience. That wasn't just true when no one else could hear me—it needed to be true in my life all the time. However, I understood it best when I lost my voice. God could hear me internally—the only way I could be heard at that time. Originally, I had believed that since I couldn't speak, I couldn't "do" my ministry. Actually, I discovered that God was asking me for my complete surrender to His will. In other words, He wanted all of me, not just my service. Without having a voice to use, I realized again that God loved me just because He loved me, not because of the great things I said about Him or the great things I did for Him.

In the process of striving for God, I had unintentionally begun to distort the truth of how I could please Him. Yet as a result of those times without a voice, I returned to the true way we can please God, which, as Job learned, is to glorify Him in every circumstance whether it makes sense or not. One very practical way to do that is to choose to take my attention off me and instead focus on God. Through prayer or singing, I can praise God for his character, love, faithfulness, mercy and compassion. I can tell Him that I know He is perfect. In other words, I can worship Him, which really just means to acknowledge His worth-ship.

Another practical way I can bring glory to God is by trusting Him. I didn't understand all that God was trying to teach me through this trial of not having a voice, so I often prayed, "My Father, I don't understand You, but I trust You." Trusting God is another important part of living a holy life, a life set apart for God's purposes. According to Christian writer Susie Hilsman, ". . . holiness means wanting to be like God so much that I will surrender everything and obey Him. He then pours Himself into me, and I come to resemble Him more."[3] A holy life is a

3 Susie Hilsman, "The Path to Holiness," *Worldwide Challenge*, July/August 1996, p. 38.

happy life, because there's tremendous freedom and joy in obedience. And God wants us to be holy, not only in our exterior performance, but in our heart attitude toward Him as well. God promises to do His part in the process, and He asks us to do our part. As you read this passage from Hebrews, see if you can distinguish our responsibilty from what God promises to do:

> Our fathers disciplined us for a little while as they thought best; but God disciplines us for our good, that we may share in His holiness. No discipline seems pleasant at the time, but painful. Later on, however, it produces a harvest of righteousness and peace for those who have been trained by it. . . . Make every effort to live in peace with all men and to be holy; without holiness no one will see the Lord (Hebrews 12:10,11,14, NIV).

Our culture and world system fights against living a holy life. "Do what is best for you," many say. "You've got to watch out for number one." Although all of God's laws do provide for us and protect us, we need to obey His laws even when we don't see how they serve our interests. This demonstrates our love and trust in our Heavenly Father. Obedience involves making conscious choices and daily decisions, each time choosing to fill our minds and hearts with God's thoughts instead of taking the media's advice or following peer pressure.

In the book of Galatians, apostle Paul wrote: "For am I

now seeking the favor of men, or of God? Or am I striving to please men? If I were still trying to please men, I would not be a bond-servant of Christ" (Galatians 1:10). He often called himself a bondservant—or slave—of Jesus Christ, because Paul's one goal was to please Jesus Christ. He chose to see Him as his master, yielding every area of his life to the Lord.

That's what holiness demands of us: surrendering completely to God. Many times that choice will be difficult, such as choosing purity when everyone else opts for the dangerous pleasures of premarital sex: "Now flee from youthful lusts, and pursue righteousness, faith, love and peace, with those who call on the Lord from a pure heart" (2 Timothy 2:22). We can give ourselves over to our emotions and our desires, or we can give ourselves completely to God.

It is wise to identify areas of our lives where we are tempted to compromise our standards. Ask God to strengthen you in those areas and develop a plan to renew your mind with His perspective. However, some will not understand your choices, sometimes not even other Christians. You may be criticized or rejected. In fact, the Bible pretty much guarantees that reaction at least once in life: "And indeed, all who desire to live godly in Christ Jesus will be persecuted" (2 Timothy 3:12).

Seek God's approval first and foremost, above all others. This is the foundation for fearing the Lord. The psalmist writes: "Teach me Your way, O Lord, and I will walk in Your truth; give me an undivided heart, that I may fear Your name" (Psalm 86:11,

NIV). When referring to God, the word *fear* has nothing to do with haunted houses and horror movies. To fear the Lord is to revere, obey and trust Him. Of course, your obedience does not increase God's love: You can do nothing to add or take away from His endless love. But through the fear of the Lord, you indicate that you care more about pleasing God than seeking the approval of others or fulfilling your own self-interests. In the long run, you are better off.

Once, when I was on the high-school basketball cheerleading squad, I saw a cute guy up in the bleachers. Completely distracted (I was watching him instead of the game), I started jumping around and cheering when I heard that a basket was scored. I was kicking my legs up and doing my best to impress that guy. Unfortunately, the other team had made the shot, and like a fool, I had been rooting for the opponent. I could have avoided that whole disaster if I had just been watching my coach and not trying to wow the cute boy in the stands. By choosing to fear the Lord, we willingly focus our attention on our heavenly Coach instead of the crowds surrounding us.

Another aspect of fearing the Lord involves hating sin. You see, God is completely and perfectly holy. Because of that, our sin (which includes anything outside of God's standard of perfection) acts like a wall of separation between us and Him. Knowing that God created us to have fellowship with Him, and knowing that our sin prevents that, we begin to understand why God hates sin so much. Since part of being holy means that we desire to be like Him, God wants us to hate sin also. Besides, having this attitude toward sin causes us to sharpen our focus on God's character and supernatural perfection. When we pursue holiness, we are drawn closer to God and also increase our desire to know Him better.

Do you desire to know the secrets of the Lord, to know what is on His heart and mind? This intimacy is promised to those who fear the Lord. Just like you tell your secrets only to your closest friends, God reveals more about Himself to the ones who draw close to Him: "The Lord confides in those who fear Him; He makes His covenant known to them" (Psalm 25:14, NIV).

The rewards are great! God is intimate with the upright (Proverbs 3:32) and the blameless are His delight (Proverbs 11:20). The Bible teaches us over and over again that the Lord loves the righteous, and that He will strengthen and support us in our desire to honor Him: "For the Lord is righteous; He loves righteousness; the upright will behold His face" (Psalm 11:7).

As we seek God and His will first, He will reveal more of Himself to us. And best of all, we will find true satisfaction in life by obeying the One who put us here in the first place. At least that's what this verse from the Psalms seems to promise: "But they who seek the Lord shall not be in want of any good thing. Come, you children, listen to me; I will teach you the fear of the Lord" (Psalm 34:10b,11).

The trendy catch-phrase "What would Jesus do?" (WWJD) has become popular, appearing on T-shirts, bracelets and hats.

Even non-Christians are sporting the four-letter brand. Although it is becoming a meaningless fashion statement, in its purest form WWJD represents an example of fearing the Lord. It reminds us to desire to please God above anyone or anything else in our lives, and prompts us to ask ourselves in every circumstance and situation what response pleases Him most.

God doesn't want us to be in want of any good thing. Isn't that amazing? He calls us His children, and therefore models how a perfect Father would raise His own kids. I have some funny stories about growing up with my dad, as you'll read in the next chapter. Because God is my Heavenly Father, He used my dad to teach me more about Himself.

chapter seven

*See how great a love the Father has bestowed upon us, that we
should be called children of God; and such we are.*

1 John 3:1a

Look Into My Father's Eyes

The noise outside my bedroom window startled me from
my sleep. Confused, I checked the time. One o'clock in the
morning? This was no summer breeze—something unusual was
going on in my parents' yard that night, and as a freshman in
high school, I wanted to know about it.

I jumped out of bed and looked through my window. All
over our backyard, the yellow glow of flashing neon construction
lights blinked back at me. I ran to the front window, and to my
amazement the front yard was covered as well with flashing lights
in every shape and size. In an instant, I figured this was the
handiwork of "Casanova Bob" and his friends.

I had been hanging around some crazy guys at the pool that summer, one of which I had a particular interest in and had actually dated a few times. My girlfriends and I nicknamed him "Casanova Bob." Needless to say, my dad was a little concerned about my interest in this young man. One week earlier I compromised my convictions about what kind of movie to see when I was out with Bob. When Dad found out, he forbade me to see him anymore. This late-night stunt, I imagined, was Bob's answer to my father's no.

Just about the time I woke up, so did Dad. He rushed out of his bedroom to discover the yard ablaze with blinking lights. You have to just take a minute and picture my dad. He is not exactly the calm, cool, collected type. Rather, I would describe him as feisty and a little bit on the reactionary side. He has the tender heart of a teddy bear, but the protective nature of a lion looking after cubs. Quite athletic, my dad played football in high school and college, and even played on a minor league baseball team. Since those days though, Dad developed arthritis, causing him to hunch over, but that definitely didn't slow him down.

I was not quite sure what was going to happen next. "Who in the world could have possibly done this?" Dad yelled. I stayed silent. Next thing I knew, he was out in the garage, rummaging around for his golf clubs. He explained to me quickly that whoever the culprit was, they would surely return, and he planned to wait patiently for him, golf club in hand. In his other hand Dad gripped his car keys.

Just like my father predicted, the boys returned to the scene of their crime. And as they drove up, Dad was ready. As soon as they got out, Dad tore after them, waving his golf club. Bob and his frightened buddies quickly got back in their Mustang to get away, so Dad jumped into his car, trailing them down the street.

Later, Bob told me, "Your dad is a wild man. He went up to 90 miles an hour chasing us." My dad gave up the chase and let the boys get away, but they got the point: My dad was not someone to mess with, especially when it involved his daughter.

Today that story makes me laugh—what a fun and crazy dad! But I am also touched by his protectiveness and care for me. I think he suspected the culprit that night, and he clearly did not want me messing around with a boy nicknamed Casanova. He and I have laughed about that episode since then, and I have thanked him for protecting me from that relationship, one that was obviously not the best for me. I didn't always receive Dad's protective involvement with such open arms, but thinking back, I can even see a glimpse of our Heavenly Father's heart. He, too, is eager to protect His children from any influence that could harm us or cause us to go down the wrong path.

Unfortunately, many of us have a hard time associating good memories with our fathers. Some have been wounded or disappointed by the man they called Dad. Others have never even met their earthly father. Yet we are told in 2 Corinthians 6:18, "'I will be a father to you, and you shall be sons and daughters to Me,' says the Lord Almighty."

Human fatherhood represents an imperfect symbol of our relationship with God, but a symbol God Himself set up. In Romans 8:15, God tells us we can cry out to Him and call him "Abba," which, in the original language, is similar to our endearing term "Daddy." What a privilege and an incredible truth, but not one that has come easily to me.

Dad was busy raising six children and working two jobs. But as a little girl, I had a tremendous desire to please him. You could find me running after him on walks outside, always wanting to keep up. I even wanted to eat the same cereal he did. I wanted him to be proud of me. Growing up with four brothers and a sister guaranteed some knockdown, drag-out fights in my house, but I took it upon myself to be the perfect daughter and the peacemaker of the family. Subconsciously, I was afraid that if I didn't live up to my perfect standard of a good daughter, then my dad would not love me. Though this wasn't really true, my little mind locked into this pattern of thought. And like most people, I carried that belief over to my understanding of God.

In my spiritual journey, I had to uncover some of those faulty belief systems that I had grown to accept. God used many ways to reveal these lies. This is the bottom line that I discovered: God's Truth is real, regardless of what your feelings may tell you. Yet we have an enemy, Satan, who wants to hinder us from believing God's truth. The enemy will keep on feeding us lies, and his only hope is that we don't contradict them by reading what God said about each lie in the Bible. Only as we begin to take these thoughts captive to the obedience of God's Word can we find victory and healing:

> The weapons we fight with are not the weapons of the world. On the contrary, they have divine power to demolish strongholds. [A stronghold is a mindset that has become embedded in our thoughts and affects our lives.] We demolish arguments and every pretension that sets itself up against the knowledge of God, and we take captive every thought to make it obedient to Christ (2 Corinthians 10:4,5, NIV).

One of the lies I bought into demanded that my worth was based on my performance. In other words, I felt that I had to meet certain standards in order for God to accept me. However, the Bible tells me that I am deeply and unconditionally loved by God. I was so excited to learn that my Heavenly Father wants to lavish His love upon you and me: "What marvelous love the Father has extended to us! Just look at it—we're called children of God! That's who we really are" (1 John 3:1, The Message).

Maybe you've believed that your sense of worth and identity hinges upon what others think of you. But God says we are totally accepted by Him once we come to Him through Jesus:

> This includes you who were once so far a way from God. You were His enemies and hated Him and were

separated from Him by your evil thoughts and actions, yet now He has brought you back as His friends. He has done this through the death on the cross of His own human body, and now as a result Christ has brought you into the very presence of God, and you are standing there before Him with nothing left against you—nothing left that He could even chide you for (Colossians 1:21,22, LB).

We all experience failure in life, but perhaps you feel unworthy of love and deserving of punishment because of your failures. You may still be blaming yourself for some mistake that you made, and you can't seem to get over that barrier. God the Father tells us that we are completely forgiven and fully pleasing to Him. If we continue to look at our past mistakes, we are rejecting God's forgiveness for us. God made Jesus, "who knew no sin to be sin on our behalf, that we might become the righteousness of God in Him" (2 Corinthians 5:21). When our Heavenly Father looks at us, He doesn't see our sin. He sees the perfect righteousness of Jesus.

Another trap or lie that we can get entangled with is that of shame, thinking we cannot change and that we are hopeless. Shame can try to hang on to us because of past experiences. For example, my eating disorder carried with it a measure of shame. I had to recognize that God had completely forgiven me, and hadn't changed His mind about me or loved me any less because of it. Maybe you lost your virginity or had an abortion, and now you feel unworthy of love. Shame frequently traps the children of divorced parents into believing that the divorce was all their fault. Victims of sexual abuse also often fall prey to the lie of shame, that somehow they think they got what was coming to them. These lies bear down on them like heavy weights. Shame is definitely detrimental to our spiritual growth, and it hinders us from experiencing God's love and forgiveness. Healing of shame begins when we identify and confess the lie that we believe about ourselves. Then we agree with God that we are His beloved child, a person of immeasurable worth, righteous and uncondemned.

In order for us to fully embrace our Father's love we have to see where we have bought into a lie. Slowly the Holy Spirit helped me recognize the false belief systems I thought to be true. I invite you to take a minute of prayer right now and ask the Holy Spirit to show you any lies you have accepted in exchange for God's truth. Then reject the lie you believed, and ask God to forgive you. Renounce (or "disown," according to Webster's) whatever first allowed that lie to take root in your heart.

It may not all become clear to you right now because often the Holy Spirit works through a process. He reveals different layers of deception to us, and as He does, we can confess and ask God to teach us His truth. As we learn these truths, we need to replace those lies with God's truth, taking them captive as we read in 2 Corinthians 10:5.

"Freedom in Christ Ministries" is a Christian organization that helps people through this spiritual process, and they helped me tremendously. As I said earlier, my eating disorder was one of the outward manifestations of my coping with the lies about my worth and value. Eventually, I began abusing alcohol as well. Since then, I have renounced the lies that I had believed about who I was, and I asked God to forgive me.

During the process, I remembered back to a time in middle school and high school when I experimented in the occult. Interestingly enough, that happened just before I began my struggle with bulimia and anorexia. My curiosity with the occult seemed innocent at the time. Some of my girlfriends wanted to play with a Ouija board. Then they started holding seances, telling fortunes, practicing hypnosis on each other and even levitating objects. I also chose to see a movie that glorified the occult and had many nightmares afterward. I understand now that these things glorify Satan, not Jesus.

And I could see the effects of those experiments on my mind: "The thief [Satan] comes only to steal, and kill, and destroy; I came that they might have life, and might have it abundantly" (John 10:10). So I had to repent and renounce each one of these experiments with the occult in order for God to bring healing to me. I know that I can experience victory over past struggles as I place my faith in Jesus, and I know this because of this verse in 1 John: "For whatever is born of God overcomes the world. And this is the victory that has overcome the world—our faith" (1John 5:4).

What a joy it was for me to go the next step, and to have

the freedom to share with my earthly father how I'd always tried to measure up and never felt completely able to be that perfect daughter. Of course, he had never expected that standard from me. We discussed my secret eating disorder and all of the emotional and physical consequences. With tears in his eyes he said, "Nancy, I never knew that, nor did I want you to feel that way."

Oftentimes our parents are not even aware of what we are experiencing. We cannot blame them because they are also imperfect, sinful people like us who also need to experience the grace and love of God. But God may want to use them in our healing process, particularly as we open up our hearts to them in God's time. Some of you may need to forgive your parents for any hurt they inflicted on you, intentional or not. That is all part of healing and growing as a Christian.

I continue to identify and confront the devil's lies with God's truth as they pop up in my daily life. And because God is compassionate as a perfect Father, He continues to extend His love to me through it all: "Just as a father has compassion on his children, so the Lord has compassion on those who fear Him" (Psalm 103:13).

My dad has a compassionate and tender side as well. I always knew he wrote love poems to Mom, but I didn't know how talented he was. As I've grown older, Dad has begun to use poems more often to express his feelings. On the occasion of my sister's birthday, she and I arranged to meet for lunch with our parents. Dad, who owns a beauty supply business, came rushing into the restaurant, his hair a little disheveled. We joked that he was not a very good advertisement for his business because his hair was sticking straight up. Anyway, he sat down with a bag in his arms.

Dad wasn't too concerned about the food. He handed my sister a poem he wrote just for her on her birthday. But then he followed it quickly by handing me a poem that he had written especially for me. My sister and I began to cry. Mom sat there with us, enjoying all the love. Dad then got out two beautifully wrapped boxes, and set them in front of my sister and me. As we opened them carefully and simultaneously, our eyes grew big as saucers. In each box was a solid gold medallion on a solid gold chain. "I have had these in a safety deposit box for 15 years," he said with a note of traceable pride in his voice, "and I've been waiting to give them to you."

Again, my mind was whisked away in thought. What an amazing picture this was of the Heavenly Father's desire to bless His children. Like my dad, God has things stored up for us, and at just the right time, He plans to shower these gifts upon us. He knows the right timing and knows when the gift will mean the most to us.

"If you then, being evil, know how to give good gifts to your children, how much more shall your heavenly Father give the Holy Spirit to those who ask Him?" (Luke 11:13). Our Heavenly Father wants to give us every good gift that we need. The greatest gift is the Holy Spirit, to assure our hearts that the

Father loves us and cares for us. And no matter what we have experienced in the way of an earthly father, we have a perfect Heavenly Father who desires to bring us into the most intimate relationship with His Son, Jesus Christ. The story of the Father's love for us is truly the greatest love story the world has ever known.

Speaking of love stories, let me tell you one that beautifully illustrates this. Shortly after my brother Dan became a Christian, he ended an immoral relationship with his girlfriend and began to trust God with every area of his life. God continued to refine Dan's character when his business in Denver collapsed. One day, after Dan had moved back home to St. Louis, my parents were taking their daily walk. They passed a woman whom Dad had noticed jogging many times before. Usually he would say to my mother, "I wish one of our sons could meet this great-looking girl." But that day, Dad jumped out without hesitation, and said, "Hi! I'm Jack, and this is Laverne. What's your name?"

"Diana," the young jogger answered, rather startled.

"We live down the street," my dad continued. "We have a son who just moved home. Would you like to meet him—well, I wondered if you'd like to meet him. He's about your age. And, on second thought, I must tell you he doesn't hang out at the bars anymore. He's a Christian now."

Diana smiled, "I'm a Christian, too."

Dad eagerly continued, "Would you like to meet him?"

Diana, startled again, replied, "Sure."

So Dad rushed back home, walking even quicker than usual,

to find Dan. "Dan, put your jogging clothes on," he yelled upstairs. "I want you to meet this girl. She lives right down the street."

Dan was surprised but quickly agreed to go. He was curious at Dad's insistence. He found the house and timidly knocked at the door. By this time, Diana was in her room getting dressed. As she looked out of the window on the second floor, she saw this prince—oh, I mean my brother. When she came down to answer the door, he said awkwardly, "I'm Dan, the one my dad told you about. Would you like to go out?"

"I guess so," Diana replied. That began a match made in heaven. Two years later, they were married.

I love that precious story because I believe God's heart was shown through my father's heart. As he was so desirous to find a bride for his son Dan, so our Heavenly Father wants to find a bride for his Son, Jesus Christ. I'm a romantic, but any theologian will tell you that the Bible is a love story involving God the Father, sending His Son to redeem us for Himself. To understand it more clearly, it helps if we know God's final goal. In Revelation it says,

> "Let us rejoice and be glad and give the glory to Him, for the marriage of the Lamb [Jesus] has come and His bride has made herself ready." And it was given to her to clothe herself in fine linen, bright and clean; for the fine linen is the righteous acts of the saints. And He said to me: "Write, 'Blessed are those who are invited

to the marriage supper of the Lamb.'" And He said to me, "These are true words of God" (Revelation 19:7-9).

When John received this revelation, he saw life's end result: the marriage supper of the Lamb. Together as believers, we make up the bridal host that will one day worship God and celebrate at this final marriage supper. The Father is involved in "wooing" a bride for His Son. His desire is to have passionate lovers of Jesus who understand their new identity as belonging to Him.

Revelation says that the bride has made herself ready, dressed in new clothing—"fine linen, bright and clean," the verse records, which symbolizes our righteousness in Jesus. Right now we are in a preparation time for the marriage ahead. When we became Christians, we got engaged, and now we're being prepared to rule and reign with Him for all eternity. That part of the plan begins once Jesus returns for us and takes us with Him to heaven. Meanwhile, we have a new identity, and our responsibility is to live that out on this earth.

Our Heavenly Father planned all of this because of His great love for us. When I look into my dad's eyes, I can see a glimpse of my Heavenly Father's heart. Growing up, I did not comprehend the gift God gave me through my dad. But now, God is helping me to fully see this model of His love through my earthly father. Let me close this chapter with a poem that I wrote for my dad on his birthday in 1998, titled "My Father's Heart."

How often tears have freely flowed
from the kindness Dad showed;
It seems his voice is always there
When I really need someone to care.
I smile to think of his special ways
And how he sacrificially spends his days;
A sense of humor he possesses
It always lightens and refreshes.
His love for Mom is so rich and dear,
It grows deeper each new year.
I love to see them in their chairs,
Taking a snooze from their cares;
Loving, sharing, growing old together,
Supporting each other in stormy weather.
My father is faithful and giving,
He's made my life fuller for living.
A glimpse of my Heavenly Father is he,
Oh, how I desire the world to see.
A precious friend He's come to be
An honor to be his daughter, that's me!

Get a Hold of This!

The Christian life would be impossible if it were up to us to carry it out on our own. Jesus knew this and told His disciples that it was better that He was going to leave them so that the Father could send the Holy Spirit to comfort, teach and guide them:

And I will ask the Father, and He will give you another Counselor to be with you forever—the Spirit of truth. The world cannot accept Him, because it neither sees Him nor knows Him. But you know Him, for He lives with you and will be in you (John 14:16,17, NIV).

Through the process of spriutal breathing, we admit our need for God's help by confessing all that we've done wrong in His eyes. Then the next step is to surrender control of our lives over to the Holy Spirit. That's where we find the power to live the Christian life!

But more than that, God is committed to conforming us to the image of Jesus Christ. Jesus said this about the Holy Spirit's purpose: "He shall praise Me and bring Me great honor by showing you My glory" (John 16:14, LB). One of the Holy Spirit's goals is to glorify Jesus and to reveal it to us.

We also have the opportunity to glorify God. Like my trip to the jail, the loss of my voice or meeting my friend George, the circumstances and people in our lives can all be agents for God's work within us. That's His wonderful promise: "For it is God who is at work in you, both to will and to work for His good pleasure" (Philippians 2:13). We can live lives that reflect a fear of the Lord.

However, God's grace is given to us not based on our merit and service, but on His faithfulness. Our prayer need not be centered around God using us as much as Him making us usable. Do you see the difference? And not to worry—He desires to use us. In fact, He's already planned to use us: "For we are His workmanship, created in Christ Jesus for good works, which God prepared beforehand, that we should walk in them" (Ephesians 2:10).

Our character and lifestyle can be a stumbling block, though, if we are not presenting ourselves to Him as vessels for honor. Let's allow God the Potter to mold us and shape us into His image. Ask Him to reveal any areas of your life that are displeasing to Him. Confess them to Him and ask His Spirit to control and empower you by faith. God desires to give you a victorious, abundant life as you experience the reality of Jesus living through you.

And no matter what you've been through—whatever pain, shame or loss you've experienced—your Heavenly Father wants to bring wholeness and healing to those wounded places. Even Jesus demonstrated a complete dependence upon His Heavenly Father's love and acceptance of Him. Run to your Heavenly Father for the grace to forgive and the power to move forward.

Take a minute right now to respond to your Heavenly Father. Invite Him into the places where you need help. Ask Him to reveal the lies you've been believing and replace them with His truth. Starting on page 188, I've reprinted a helpful list of Scripture references about your identity as a Christian. Take a moment to read them and meditate on them.

Decide who you will reach out to for accountability and prayer. Thank God for filling you and empowering you with His Holy Spirit. You are not alone on this journey—He is your Helper and Guide!

A place to write your thoughts:

Part Three

Called to Partnership
With Him

*For we are God's workmanship, created in
Christ Jesus to do good works, which God
prepared in advance for us to do.*

Ephesians 2:10, (NIV)

chapter eight

*Delight yourself in the Lord; and He will give you the
desires of your heart. Commit your way to the Lord,
trust also in Him, and He will do it.*

Psalm 37:4

Honeymoon With Jesus

My heart was pounding fast. I could hardly believe my ears.

Six months earlier I had prayed a secret prayer just between Jesus and me. "Lord," I prayed, "it's my desire to go to Jerusalem to learn more about you." Tucking this dream away in my prayer journal, I thought God would answer some day, way later, like when I was retired. Less than a year after my prayer, I received a phone call from two of my closest friends, Pam and Bill.

"Are you sitting down?" they asked. *Were they going to have another baby?* I wondered. *Or maybe something was wrong.* I gulped.

"Nancy," my friend said, "We want to take you to Israel with us, all expenses paid!"

Even though they were my close friends, I had not told them about my secret desire to go to Israel. Only Jesus knew. This was a special gift from the Lord, and even the timing was perfect. I was turning 30 years old, and I was still single. I was content as a single woman, knowing that God had a special plan for my life. But I had joked around with the Lord, telling Him how I certainly would enjoy a honeymoon. It seemed that this special occasion was the honeymoon I was waiting for, and so I anticipated a week of intimacy with Jesus. It all seemed perfectly designed for me.

As the time drew closer to go on the trip, my friends Pam and Bill, who had so graciously invited me to join them, discovered that Pam was pregnant after all. This was very good news, but it unfortunately also meant that they could no longer go to Israel. Still, they insisted I go alone. Everyone else on the trip was paired up in twos, so I decided my partner would be Jesus. I pictured Him as my personal guide sitting beside me on the bus. Reflecting on His life, death and resurrection in the very places He once walked caused me to fall more deeply in love with Him. What tender memories!

My blond hair and blue eyes drew some attention in Israel. I actually received several marriage proposals, one from a young Arab teen-ager willing to throw in 50 camels with the deal. Can you imagine that? My fellow tourists were insulted he did not offer more. They said I was worth at least 200 camels!

Needless to say, I came home still single, but my

"honeymoon with Jesus" has since become a tradition. Every year the Lord and I choose a special time to get away, just Him and me. It's been a delightful surprise to see what rich and creative weekends have come out of that desire to be with Him.

On one such weekend with the Lord, I was walking along Newport Beach in California, meditating on Him and on the privilege of my intimate partnership with Him. As I stood in the sand and watched the sun sink into the horizon, the reality of oneness with God began to settle in my heart in a fresh way. The Bible parallels the relationship between a husband and a wife with the relationship between Christ and the church. Standing before the sunset I reflected on this intimate thought of being the very bride of Christ, of being prepared to one day rule and reign as His partner throughout all eternity. I experienced an overwhelming sense of anticipation for the moment we would be united as one, together for all eternity. What an awesome thought!

While the colors of the sunset stretched over the ocean, I thought about Paul's words in the book of Colossians:

Since you became alive again, so to speak, when Christ arose from the dead, now set your sights on the rich treasures and joys of heaven where He sits beside God in the place of honor and power. Let heaven fill your thoughts; don't spend your time worrying about things down here. You should have as little desire for this world as a dead person does. Your real life is in heaven with Christ and God. And when Christ who is our real life comes back again you will shine with Him and share in all His glories (Colossians 3:1-4, LB).

Consider with me what this means, as I did that peaceful evening on the beach. You and I (assuming that you have received Jesus Christ as your Savior and Lord) are co-heirs with Jesus Christ. Everything He gained through the cross is available to us, namely our partnership with Him for all eternity: "For our citizenship is in heaven, from which also we eagerly wait for a Savior, the Lord Jesus Christ" (Philippians 3:20).

If, indeed, my citizenship is in heaven, then my home is heaven and I'm just a visitor here on this earth. Suddenly, it became so clear to me that I was here on a mission that God the Father had planned before I was born.

To celebrate my 35th birthday, I prayed again, asking the Lord to provide another special honeymoon. It was as if He asked me, *Where would you like to go?* Without blinking an eye, I silently prayed, "Lord, you know I've always dreamed of going to Hawaii."

Several months later, my job required that I travel to Guam and the Micronesian Islands so that I could train youth leaders and help begin a youth ministry there. When I received my travel itinerary, I discovered we were stopping in Hawaii to change planes. Amazing! After working with Cindy, my travel agent, I was able to arrange a stopover on the way home at no extra charge. My dream really wasn't impossible to God!

I spent five days in Hawaii praising God for all He is to me. I reveled in His intimate love for me and thoroughly enjoyed a needed rest in His presence.

Every morning I would walk and talk with Him on the beach. One morning, I asked, "Lord, what is my ultimate purpose for being here on earth? I would love to be with You now, but I know You have me here for a very specific reason."

It was as if His Spirit whispered in my ear, *Nancy, I have created you for My glory!* I was a bit surprised at the simplicity of His response.

He wasn't asking me to "do" some big dramatic thing, just simply to "be" His unique creation. And best of all, that brings glory to my Creator as He leads me into His specific will. I have returned to the words of His whispered answer many times. So often, I think that my value comes from what I have accomplished, even if my motives in accomplishing the task were for God's purposes and not mine. It blows my mind when I remember that Jesus finds glory in me just because He created me.

Did you know that you have been created by God to serve a unique purpose? You've been hearing it since kindergarten, but it is true that no one else is exactly like you. And more than just the fact that no one shares your fingerprint, or your hair color or voice or body shape, God has designed you to reflect Him spiritually in a way that no one else ever can. Before you were born, God had already developed a course for your life, just as He has for mine! Consider this: "All the days ordained for me were written in Your book before one of them came to be" (Psalm 139:16, NIV). He has equipped you with certain gifts and abilities, then arranged your upbringing and circumstances to help fulfill your divine destiny.

How can each of us discover and experience the particular plan God has in mind for us? By getting to know the One who created us, the One ". . . who has called [us] into fellowship with His Son, Jesus Christ . . ." (1 Corinthians 1:9, NIV). However, our ability to walk in God's plan for us is directly related to the depth of our relationship with Him. The more we get to know the Lord, the deeper our dependency on Him becomes, and the better we are able to discern where He is leading us (John 10:27). As we follow Him, we can then be confident that we will fulfill our ultimate purpose in life.

One of the most exciting aspects of an intimate love relationship with Jesus is His sharing His heart with you. As you grow in your devotion to Christ, He will reveal more of His heart to you. We are promised in James 4:8, "Draw near to God, and He will draw near to you." Christian teacher Kay Arthur tells a story that adds a word picture to this idea. She and her husband were watching a medical program on television about open heart surgery: "Two human hearts were laying side by side. Each was beating at different rhythms. The surgeon moved them together, until the tissue of one heart touched the other. Suddenly, both assumed the same rhythm."[1]

How similar to our relationship with God. When we draw close to Him, our heart begins to beat with the things that are on God's heart. He cares deeply about the needs of people. His heart is broken over many who are searching and alone, not knowing that they have a Heavenly Father who loves and cares for them.

We've been sent into the world to reflect God's love to them, and to introduce them to their Savior. We are privileged to be chosen, but even more exciting is the fact that we have been chosen with a mission. That mission was summarized in the final instructions which Jesus gave His disciples before returning to heaven. Today many call those words the Great Commission:

> All authority has been given to Me in heaven and on earth. Go therefore and make disciples of all the nations, baptizing them in the name of the Father and the Son and the Holy Spirit, teaching them to observe all that I commanded you; and lo, I am with you always, even to the end of the age (Matthew 28:18-20).

Even though God does all the work by changing the person and preparing his or her soul, I still call it a partnership because He's invited me to share His message with my lips and to display His love through my life's actions. As Jesus said in the Great Commission verse, He promises to be with us in the incredible endeavor. But His heart of compassion for the lost and His zeal for doing His Father's will has become mine. This is probably one of the most joyful aspects of our intimate relationship with Jesus. We get to be a partner with Him in His mission to seek and save the lost.

God grants me that privilege every day as I am in tune with Him, even when I was in Hawaii. One day on the beach, while relishing the beauty of the palm trees and the smell of the plumeria blossoms, I couldn't help but notice all the couples walking hand in hand, experiencing the joys of romance. For a while, it intrigued me, but soon my emotions kicked in. "Lord, it's wonderful that I'm here with You enjoying all of this, but there are times when I wish You had some skin and bones."

I began to feel lonely, and all of a sudden, I started to cry. I didn't want to spoil this intimate time with God by feeling sorry for myself. After all, I was on a honeymoon with Jesus in Hawaii! So I got up, ran into the ocean, and decided to swim as far out as I could. I've had lifeguards in the past blow their whistle to keep me from swimming out too far, but there was no lifeguard around this time. I swam and swam until the salty water replaced my tears and my joy returned. Stopping to catch my breath, I noticed a guy on a kickboard staring at me. I began to tread water when he asked, "Who are you anyway?"

"Well," I answered, "Do you really want to know?"

"Yes, I've been watching you swim so fast and so long," the stranger said. "I've never seen anyone who doesn't seem to get tired. It's amazing."

"I used to train dolphins," I explained, "and I love to swim in the ocean. But you asked who I am. I happen to be an ambassador."

"An ambassador?"

"Yes," I said. "I go all over the world and tell people that God loves them."

"Oh, my gosh, I can't believe it," he said. "Just last night, I was on a camp-out with all these guys and I went up to this mountain late at night looking at the stars. I asked God to show me if He was real."

Amazed at God's timing, I answered, "And I'm here to tell you, YES! He is real, and He loves you and has a special plan for you. And He sent me all the way from America and out into the middle of the ocean to tell you this!"

Needless to say, Max was a little surprised by my response. But he and I became great friends. After swimming back to shore, we arranged to meet at his bread shop, which he owned. There, I told Max all about Jesus, the Bread of Life, and he gave me six loaves of delicious Hawaiian bread to take with me. The next Sunday, Max came to a church with me where he prayed and received Jesus Christ as his Lord and Savior.

How thrilling it is to be intimately acquainted with the Lord, so that He can sovereignly lead us to respond to the heart cry of people wherever we are. Even out in the ocean!

It blows my mind how God cares about lost people

searching for Him. He promises to reveal Himself to those who are sincerely seeking to know the truth, like Max: "And you will seek Me and find Me, when you search for Me with all your heart" (Jeremiah 29:13).

Sometimes our intimacy with the Lord is challenged by other attractions, but God desires that we would choose Him above other things and keep Him in first place. In other words, God wants to be our "first love." We must choose to prioritize God or surrender our first love to something else. As the apostle Paul wrote,

I am jealous for you with a godly jealousy. I promised you to one husband, to Christ, so that I might present you as a pure virgin to Him. But I am afraid that just as Eve was deceived by the serpent's cunning, your minds may somehow be led astray from your sincere and pure devotion to Christ (2 Corinthians 11:2,3, NIV).

Think about a relationship that is very special to you. You want to be with that person. You would gladly choose spending time with him or her before doing anything else. That is one way we show the Lord our love and give Him the opportunity to share His heart and secrets with us.

But sometimes, we surrender our first love for something else. Even a relationship with another person can take us away from God. I can think of several relationships in my life where the Lord asked me to choose Him over those men, asking me to make Jesus my first love.

One man in particular became very important to me. I knew in my heart that I had put him on a pedestal. While praying and reading in my Bible, I came across Psalm 118:8,9: "It is better to trust in the Lord than to put confidence in man. It is better to trust in the Lord than to put confidence in princes" (NKJ).

The Holy Spirit revealed to me that I had made this man to be a prince in my eyes. He had taken the place that only the Lord deserves. Through my tears, I yielded that relationship to the Lord and said "yes" to God's will above my own, knowing and believing that His will was perfect. I have never regretted any choice that I have made to choose Jesus as my first love. In fact, I delight in the thought that He desires my love so much that He would be jealous for my affection.

I don't mean to imply that you can only choose God as your first love by living a life of singleness. That is not the issue. The issue is choosing to make Jesus your first love, and letting Him decide when and with whom you are to have a relationship. Only He can meet the deepest needs of your heart. Always guard your heart from idols. An idol is anything that we surrender our attention and affections to in the place of Jesus Christ. Relationships, like money and power, can became idols and can hinder your first love with Jesus.

Why don't you take a personal inventory of your relationship with the Lord? How are you cultivating your first love with Jesus? Are you getting to know Him better and better through spending time with Him? Have you treasured His Word like a personal love letter written by Him for you? Do you meditate on His character and His ways?

Maybe the place you need to begin is to ask Him to show you more of His personal love for you: "The Lord your God is in your midst, a victorious warrior. He will exult over you with joy, He will be quiet in His love, He will rejoice over you with shouts of joy" (Zephaniah 3:17). Think about a God who gets excited about you. How can you resist wanting to develop an intimate relationship with Him? It simply takes time and desire, "for where your treasure is, there will your heart be also" (Matthew 5:21).

Why not make Him your treasure? You are His treasured bride. That was how I felt when I first wrote the words to the following poem in the pages of my journal:

What joy and pure delight
Is in my heart tonight:
To share this intimate love,
Now and forever above.
I revel in my royalty—
a priceless responsibility.
Fill my soul with fresh fire;

Consume me with passion and desire
For Your glory to be shown,
Illuminating Your throne.
Oh King of the Universe,
You've broken the enemy's curse.
Cause the nations to see
Jesus died to set them free!
Teach me new revelation,
Lift me to a higher elevation.
As I'm lost in wonder and awe
That I'm delivered from the law—
Grace, grace, God's grace
Captivates me as I seek Your face.
How I long to fully display
My Father's love in a deeper way;
For Jesus, my beloved Lover,
My Deliverer, Savior and my Cover,
You're the Bright Morning Star
When hope seems so far.
By the power of Your name,
I'm released from all shame;

I'm dancing with joy
That none can destroy.

All worship to You;
My devotion is due;
I bow low at Your feet,
And You lift me to my seat
In the heavenly place
To gaze into Your face!
Oh Jesus, don't allow me to miss
Your intimate kiss;
Your Beloved Bride, Nancy

Loving God with all your heart, soul and mind sums up what it means to be His disciple, and it is also the mark of being His bride. I want every day to be a honeymoon with Jesus, and it can be, as long as I walk closely with Him. One day, sooner than we may think, we'll be united with Him forever. I want to be ready.

chapter nine

We are Christ's ambassadors. God is using us to speak to
you: we beg you, as though Christ Himself were here
pleading with you, receive the love He offers you—
be reconciled to God.

2 *Corinthians* 5:20 *(LB)*

Adventures
of an Ambassador

"**H**i, my name is Peg, and I'm your driver." I jumped into the back seat of the airport limousine, thankful to be flying home. I was thankful the limo was on time picking me up, but my driver wasn't a bearer of good news: "I want to let you know that a lot of the planes at the Chicago airport have been slowed down because of the snow, so I can't guarantee your plane will leave on time. I still suggest waiting at the airport—eventually you'll get home. With this snow you just never know what may happen."

Well, that sounds dimly promising, I thought. But after a busy week of training with co-workers from around the nation, I was tired and could not wait to return home. Peg and I began to talk and pretty soon, in the congested traffic, she opened up to me about her distressing life. It always amazes me that people will share so much with a total stranger, but then, they are often starving for love and attention, and someone's genuine interest works like a key unlocking their heart's door. What's behind that door is often very sad and full of pain, or sometimes it's covered over with spiritual indifference and self-sufficiency. But Jesus sees through it all. He knocks at that barred-up door by using His messengers of love, a privilege that belongs to you and me.

Peg's honesty and openness made me feel as if I had known her for a long time. Actually, by the time we finally made it to the airport, I had! But, like my delayed commute, our setbacks often become God's divine opportunities. In fact, Peg was an answer to my morning prayer. As usual, I had begun my day expressing my availability to God. "I'm Your servant, Lord," I prayed. "Fill me with Your heart, Your mind, Your words, Your Spirit. Use me for your glory today. And please make up for my weaknesses, Lord!" He answered me, as He is so faithful to do, on the way to the airport.

We waited in traffic for an hour and a half, so I was able to tell Peg about my relationship with Jesus Christ, explaining how she, too, could know Him personally. In fact, cars came to a complete standstill because of the bad weather, so I could actually lead her step by step through Jesus' message of hope and good news, using an evangelistic booklet called the *Four Spiritual Laws*.

The angels must have held up traffic so they could party without distraction, because, there in the limousine, Peg became a Christian, surrendering her life to Jesus Christ's control: "In the same way, I tell you there is joy in the presence of the angels over one sinner who repents" (Luke 15:10). Peg now had her own Problem-solver who would be with her forever. What joy I felt along with the angels, and of course, our Lord Himself.

When we pulled up to the airport, Peg and I hugged and said goodbye, exchanging phone numbers and addresses. Then I was off running, hoping I would not miss my plane. Jogging through the airport I reminded the Lord that I really did want to get home, and the sooner, the better. Again, He answered my prayers: Even though I arrived late at the gate, my plane was just boarding because of a delay. I thanked my Heavenly Father for the favor, and handed the agent my ticket.

God must have a sense of humor or take great delight in surprises, because He certainly fills my life with the unexpected! I found my seat, and leaned back to get comfortable, only to hear the pilot's voice over the intercom.

"Due to the snowstorm, there is a backup on the runway and 74 planes are in front of us. We'll be waiting until we can be cleared for takeoff. We're sorry for the inconvenience. We will be serving complimentary drinks while we wait."

What? Seventy-four planes? I never knew so many could fit on one runway! I had to laugh, knowing the Lord must have some reason for the unimaginable delay. But there, sitting next to me, was the reason: another woman whom God had prepared long before this moment. She, too, wanted to meet Jesus in a personal way, and with an hour to kill before takeoff, I had the privilege of explaining how she could do that. What an indescribable joy I experienced when she too prayed with me and received God's gift of salvation.

As His ambassador, we can view every one of life's circumstances as an opportunity to serve the Lord. Since I travel a lot, I get to do that every time I meet someone on the airplane, and God introduces me to all kinds of people. What a joy to introduce them to the Love of my life: Jesus. I remember the time a bronzed bodybuilder in shorts and a muscle shirt squeezed through the narrow airplane aisle and sat down in my row. He looked like a model from one of those weight-lifting magazines.

After offering him part of my meal, (I was afraid he'd be undernourished with airplane portions) he declined, saying, "No, thank you; I had seven breakfasts on my last flight." I later discovered this was Mr. Florida, aspiring to become Mr. Universe! I told him about the God who created the universe and all those in it, including him. Sometimes, the people I speak with already know Jesus and have committed their lives to Him, as was the case with Mr. Florida. But I can't tell whether someone is a Christian just by looking at him or her, and besides, speaking about my Savior helps to build my spiritual muscles. Best of all, that little conversation may change their lives forever. In Mr. Florida's case, God used me to encourage him to continue standing against the pressures of steroid-use in his sport, and to fight compromises of His convictions through the power of the Holy Spirit.

Even though I want to take seriously my privileged responsibility as God's ambassador, I don't always feel the most likely candidate to represent Him. That happened the day I was sitting on a plane, reviewing material for teens about sexual abstinence and considering it for the high school ministry where I work. The lady seated next to me seemed very unhappy and rather tough-looking. She was reading material published by the National Organization for Women (NOW) on why abortion should be legalized for teens. Struck by how different her material was from mine, I thought, *This had to be a divine placement.* So I began to pray for God to open a door if He wanted to use me to love her.

As our meal was served, the woman brusquely asked, "So what do you do, anyway?" She had obviously noticed my reading materials.

"I help young people understand how they can have a personal relationship with God," I answered.

"I thought so," she said. "One of those religious people."

"No," I quickly responded. "I'm not religious at all."

Just to make sure she got it, I even paused. Then I continued, "But I do have a relationship with Someone who has changed my life."

That led into a two-hour discussion about Jesus, the person who elevated the role of women more than any other in history. I don't think she had ever thought about Jesus in this way, and she gradually grew more curious and interested.

Well into our conversation, I realized that I had never asked her name. I managed to cover my surprise at her response. She was a woman of great leadership in NOW, and I had already been praying specifically for her on my prayer list long before we had met. When I had begun praying for her, I knew only that she had significant influence over the lives of many women, and wondered if she had ever heard God's message of hope. I had no idea that God might use me to act as part of His answer to my prayers.

Yet there she was, sitting next to me, en route to be the keynote speaker at a NOW convention in San Diego. At the end of our conversation, I explained how she could know Jesus personally, believing that one day she would want to know how to become a Christian. Because of our time together, she willingly listened and accepted the booklet that I gave her. I still pray for her to this day, and often wonder if she has since given her life over to Jesus.

You may not fly on airplanes as much as I do, but what about your neighborhood, campus or job? Wherever you spend each day, God wants to invade it with His presence and power. He delights in making ordinary days supernatural. "'You are My witnesses,' declares the Lord, 'And my servant whom I have chosen, in order that you may know and believe Me, and understand that I am He'" (Isaiah 43:10a).

You can begin living out your role as God's witness by

making a prayer list of family members, friends, neighbors and co-workers. By praying specifically for the people who are part of your everyday environment, you can literally capture your campus or community for Christ. God alone can bring people to Himself, but He can use us to be His hands, feet and mouth!

I pray specifically for others on a regular basis while walking throughout my apartment complex. I call it "prayer walking" because I spend that time telling Jesus about the teen-agers, children, older couples and maintenance men that I've met in my neighborhood. And for each person, I ask God to call him or her to Himself. God is so faithful to hear our prayers; all we do is cooperate with Him in His saving work. What joy and expectation we can have as His ambassadors, because it's His plan and purpose. We've been chosen for this mission!

For "whoever will call upon the name of the Lord will be saved." How then shall they call upon Him in whom they have not believed? And how shall they believe in Him whom they have not heard? And how shall they hear without a preacher? And how shall they preach unless they are sent? Just as it is written, "How beautiful are the feet of those who bring glad tidings of good things!" (Romans 10:13-15).

That verse reminds me of a letter I received during my summer as a dolphin trainer. After one of my shows, someone handed me a message from a secret admirer. As I opened it, I was surprised to find a five-page letter describing in great details the beauty of my feet. Now granted, this man must have been a little strange, but he knew more than he realized. According to that passage in Romans 10, I *do* have beautiful feet, because they have been entrusted with God's good news.

How beautiful are your feet? Have you experienced the joy of sharing Jesus with others? Pray for God's heart and His eyes to see people the way He does. When we read the following verse in Matthew, we understand how God sees people:

> Jesus went through all the towns and villages, teaching in their synagogues, preaching the good news of the kingdom and healing every disease and sickness. When He saw the crowds, he had compassion on them, because they were harassed and helpless, like sheep without a shepherd (Matthew 9:35,36, NIV).

I have a friend named Josh, a junior at Mountain Ridge High School in Phoenix, who is on the football team and captain of the wrestling team. Josh wanted his teammates to come to know Christ, so he began to pray for them. The Lord prompted Josh to organize an outreach where he invited all his friends, and there he explained the gospel to them. After hearing about a personal relationship with God through Jesus Christ, 14 of the 19 guys prayed and received Christ into their lives. Josh didn't want to leave them hanging spiritually, so he began a Bible study to help his friends grow in their newfound faith. Josh has been a great influence on his teammates. He attributes it to the power of God through prayer. In fact, he has eternally influenced many of them, because he willingly accepted the adventure of being God's ambassador.

So did another high-school student named Ashleigh. As she was praying for her high school in Plano, Texas, she and her friends heard about the way God was using the *JESUS* film around the world. The video shows the life of Christ through the words of Luke, and at the end viewers get the chance to pray and invite Jesus into their lives. The film is so powerful that it has been translated into more than 450 languages—more translations than any other film ever made.

Ashleigh and her friends thought, *Why can't we show this at our high school?* So with prayer and boldness, they scheduled a meeting with their high school principal. God answered their prayers, and the principal allowed them to host an evening assembly at the school. Using posters and announcements over the PA system, they invited anyone to come. "I'll never forget the faces of the people there that night," Ashleigh said, "Hindus, Muslims, teachers and friends. Not only were people's lives changed, but the gospel of Jesus Christ was proclaimed at our school."

I also have some friends from Cypress Creek High School in Orlando, Florida, who were concerned about their girlfriends on campus getting sexually involved before thinking it through.

We organized a girls' sexuality panel on which several girls shared their experiences and some of their past failures. The girls also explained how God rebuilt their self-esteem and gave them a reason to say no to sexual pressures. I had the privilege of sharing the gospel afterward, to show that Jesus forgives any mistake we've made, nailing our shame to the Cross. Two precious teenage girls opened up their hearts to Jesus that day.

God can use us to lead our family members to Him as well. But sometimes it is even harder to witness to them than to strangers or friends. When my younger sister was in high school, she kept a messy room. The problem was, Karen and I shared the room, and seeing clothes strewn everywhere used to drive me crazy. My solution in the past was to crumple them all up in a grocery bag and shove them into her closet. *That'll teach her to be neat!* I thought.

But then I went away to college and became a Christian. On spring break, I returned home for a week and asked God how to reach her. I heard the Holy Spirit answer, *If you really love Karen and want to demonstrate My love to her, then you'll clean her room for her.*

I resisted at first, but I finally yielded to God's leading. For the rest of the week, I made her bed and hung up her clothes in the closet instead of burrowing everything away in a bag or yelling at her. Naturally, Karen noticed.

"What's happened to you, Nancy?" she asked. Accepting her invitation to explain this change in my life, I told her again how Jesus had transformed my heart, and I told her how I had hoped that she too would desire a personal relationship with Jesus. Karen prayed with me and received Jesus as her Savior and Lord. That marks one of my all-time favorite days of my life. I love my sister, and can't imagine spending eternity without her! (By the way, she outgrew the messy stage. Today she is an amazingly neat and organized woman.)

We need to remember that people, including many of our friends and family, need to hear about Jesus and His good news. If you will take the initiative to share that message with them, it would meet the most important need they have. The apostle Paul said he was not ashamed of the good news of Jesus Christ (Romans 1:16), and we shouldn't be, either.

We're not responsible for changing people's hearts: that is God's job. According to Bill Bright, whom I think of as a spiritual mentor, successful witnessing is "taking the initiative in the power of the Holy Spirit and leaving the results to God." But being prepared to talk about our faith and learning how to give it away *is* our responsibility as Christians. I recommend getting some training to help you feel confident and equipped to be His witness. Campus Crusade for Christ offers many tools designed to help you, which you can find at your local Christian bookstore. Or ask your pastor about your church's evangelism committee. Jesus said to His disciples, "The harvest is plentiful but the workers are few. Therefore, beseech the Lord of the harvest to send out workers into His harvest" (Matthew 9:37,38).

All over the world, God is using ordinary people to reap a spiritual harvest. More than 140,000 people are coming to know Christ everyday around the world, according to mission experts. In all my 23 years of knowing Jesus and participating in evangelism, I've never experienced such hunger and responsiveness to His message of truth as now. God may be calling you to be one of His chosen laborers to go into the harvest full time, to devote all your energy toward His kingdom work. It is an honor for me to give the King of kings my total allegiance and my complete focus of attention.

But we are all full-time laborers in His eyes, even if God doesn't call you to make it your life's work. That is what this verse in Acts means:

> But you shall receive power when the Holy Spirit has come upon you; and you shall be My witnesses both in Jerusalem, and in all Judea and Samaria, and even to the remotest part of the earth (Acts 1:8).

Since Jesus made us His witnesses, ask Him what He would have for you. Begin with your family, campus or neighborhood (kind of like your "Jerusalem"), and pray along with me for the Lord of the harvest to send out His workers today all over the world, into the harvest. Step out in faith and believe Him to use you where He's placed you today! He's waiting and eager to lead you in the adventure of being His ambassador. Your "Jerusalem" today, the world tomorrow!

My family: Dan, Keith, Mark, Jack, me, Dad, Mom, Karen

Me (top right) with my kabin kampers at Kamp Kakakomo.

Everyone called Mike "Ken-Doll." Since he couldn't get Barbie to go to the prom, he took "Skipper" instead.

The Mistress of Maritime Merriment in action at a dolphin show at Six Flags

Wild Bill and I make a grand entrance at the college union Christmas party as Santa and his elf.

*Making a fashion statement in London with my "classy" jumper,
on my way to the House of Commons.*

*Uncle Francis lived to celebrate his 81st birthday, here in
Budapest, Hungary, even though he was willing to die for Jesus.*

In a Muslim country, God led me to an empty dress shop so I could tell this woman about Jesus.

Everywhere we went in South Africa, we found people hungry for God. Men, women and children walked miles to visit this church under a tent in Swaziland.

In Trinidad high schools, I was allowed to share the gospel freely during class.

While training youth leaders in India, I met friends who shared my passion for the youth of their nation.

Meeting Moses in the Korean prayer cave.

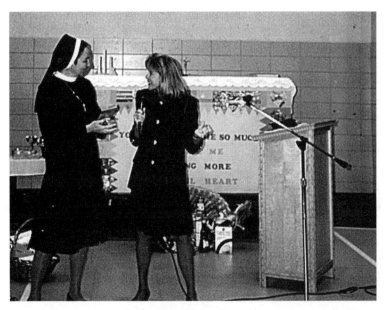

I returned to my high school in St. Louis, Missouri, to share the heart of Jesus at Cor Jesu Academy.

Imagine, hundreds of high school students gathered together for an entire weekend—just to pray!

A breath taking view in the Swiss Alps.

chapter ten

And whatever you ask in My name, that will I do,
that the Father may be glorified in the Son. If you
ask Me anything in My name, I will do it.

John 14:13-14

Scaling the Prayer Mountain

"Did you lose your checkbook, Nancy?" asked Michael, the maintenance man at my apartment complex.

Caught off guard, I thought for a moment. "No, I don't think so," I answered, a little confused.

"I think you did, Nancy," Michael said with a big smile. "This one has got to be yours." He lifted up a small checkbook cover and showed it to me. Seeing the plastic billfold stuffed with index cards, I realized Michael did have something that belonged to me, but it wasn't my checkbook. When I find a Bible verse stating a promise from God, I often write it on an index card and put it inside the checkbook folder that Michael was holding. I see those promises like blank checks: God gave them to us to cash in on. As Christians, we are rich, with all our Heavenly Father's resources at our disposal. We need only to ask.

Michael said he found the billfold by the pool. I must have left it there after a time of prayer. "Michael," I asked, "what can I pray for you today?"

Prayer is such a privilege—a chance for us to tell God anything. But it hasn't always been that high on my priority list. As you know, I like to be at the center of the action, and I used to look at prayer as very behind-the-scenes. Boy, did the Lord have a lot to teach me!

He used Youth Congress '85 to do some of that teaching. This large gathering of youth was a joint effort between Student Venture (of Campus Crusade for Christ) and Campus Life (of Youth for Christ), in cooperation with hundreds of churches and youth ministries across America. The leaders of these organizations, of whom I am one, had planned and dreamed about an event like it for so long. When our dream came together, 16,000 young people gathered in Washington, D.C., to be trained, challenged and sent out to make a difference in their world.

I had been asked to coordinate the prayer emphasis for the event. But as I said earlier, I wanted to be in the center of the action, so I wasn't sure about this prayer role. However, after talking to Jesus about it, He gave me such a vision for the role of prayer that I realized I had been entrusted with a very strategic role. In fact, through some study, I became convinced that the highest privilege we have as children of God is to participate in partnership with God through prayer.

I understood it even more clearly while reading about the church in Korea, which is the largest growing collection of Christian believers in the world. More than 20 churches are planted every day, and established churches are also doing well. On a trip to Asia, I attended Central Assembly in Seoul (David Yonggi Cho's church) with 750,000 others. In fact, Seoul—Korea's capital—is home to 10 of the 20 largest congregations in the world, and 40 percent of the citizens of that city profess to be Christians.

The secret to this immense spiritual growth can be found in the diligent prayers of the Korean believers. Many Christians go to places called "prayer mountains" for prayer retreats. Literally up in rocky crags and hills, these prayer mountains provide a place for men and women to pray for long periods of time individually and collectively. The Korean Christians have claimed their nation for God.

I decided to scale a prayer mountain during my visit to the country, and I'll never forget it. On my way up the mountain, I passed three crosses depicting Christ' sacrificial death. I proceeded to the top of the mountain and came to a cave, reminding me of His resurrection—the event in history that gives power to our prayers. I could hear loud echoes coming from within the cave, and based on all the noise, I figured many were praying inside. However, there was only one man within the cave; he was just praying with a lot of passion. I experienced earth-shaking prayer that day as I prayed along with this Christian man from Africa. Afterward, he told me that his first name was, believe it or not, Moses. I not only met with God on the mountain that day, but "Moses" as well!

Later in my trip, I sat in the Korean Olympic stadium and witnessed 80,000 young people dedicate themselves to the fulfillment of the Great Commission (Matthew 28:18-20). It was pouring rain, but that did not dampen their zeal or incredible fervor. These young people pledged their lives to go to nations of the world that still have not heard about Jesus' love and life-changing message. As I was leaving the stadium, I talked with a group of Korean high school students. I told them about my vision for the youth of the world and my prayer that this generation would declare the praises of God throughout the world. My new friends hugged me and promised me that they would pray for America.

The Koreans' example so challenged me that when I returned, I found my own prayer mountain several blocks from my home in San Diego. Early in the morning I would spend special time of prayer with the Lord anyway, so I decided to climb my mini-mountain and pray up there. Unlike the one I visited in Korea, this mountain was marked with empty beer bottles, cigarettes and graffiti painted on rocks. Still, these served as vivid reminders of the desperate condition of our nation, and in particular, the needs of America's youth. There, my burden for spiritual awakening among young people deepened, and my vision for prayer's effectiveness grew.

Up on my prayer mountain, I often prayed specifically for a high school campus near my home known for satanic activity. In fact, a police officer spoke with my pastor, concerned for this high school and the potential suicides that often occur in the presence of satanic activity.

One early morning, making my way atop "Prayer Mountain," I discovered I was not the only one there. It looked as if I'd crashed an all-night party. The first guy I met was skinny, with a drawn face and sunken eyes. He was dressed completely in black, and his hair was shaved into a mohawk. I introduced myself to him, and he told me his name was Shadow Cat. His friends explained to me that he got the nickname from all the black cats he had killed. Shadow Cat appeared to be the leader in the group of teens, and he and I developed a rapport. I was joking with him, and yet able to be direct with him about his need for a relationship with God.

I believe God allowed Shadow Cat to be open with me that morning because the whole encounter had been preceded by prayer. Many times I had climbed that prayer mountain to pray against the satanic activity in my local high school, and here God sent me to talk with one of the leaders, to serve as an answer to my own prayers. I discovered Shadow Cat's real name was Paul. We got to know each other better, and I told Paul very strongly that God had a destiny for his life. I explained to him that it was not by accident that God sent me up to the top of the mountain to tell him about God's deep love and care for him. Paul listened very intently. Later, he even attended my church youth group: They had also been praying for him.

After our first morning meeting, Paul and I had some very open conversations about his life and the gospel. His father divorced his mother and moved to New York, and shortly after that, Paul also moved. He did not fully embrace Jesus in my presence, but I believe with all my heart that he will come into God's kingdom. I continue to pray for my friend Paul, and pray someday that I will meet him atop the mountain in the Holy City of Heaven.

There are many others like him who are open to the gospel, crying out for a supernatural answer to life's demands. They are just waiting for someone to tell them about Jesus Christ, and I am praying that person—maybe you—hears God's call to speak.

The Lord gives us a model of how prayer changed a corrupt culture in the book of Daniel in the Bible. Daniel was probably in his late teens when he and his friends were taken captive and made to serve in King Nebuchadnezzar's ungodly court. Eventually, the king promoted Daniel and gave him authority to rule over the whole province of Babylon. Through it all, Daniel honored God above everything and everyone else, even when it jeopardized his life.

The book of Daniel contains several exciting stories about that, but one of the most famous pieces of history in the Old

Testament is Daniel's decision to pray at all costs. Daniel was still in charge and much older at the time, under the rule of King Darius. Several leaders became jealous of Daniel's distinguished record of honor and favor with the king. They wanted to make him look bad: "Then these men said, 'We shall not find any ground of accusation against this Daniel unless we find it against him with regard to the law of his God'" (Daniel 6:5). So they convinced King Darius to set a royal statute and firm decree against praying to anyone but the king. All perpetrators would be thrown into a den of lions. In order to seal Daniel's fate, the leaders got the command from the king in writing.

The best part of the story is that Daniel knew there would be grave consequences to disobeying the king, but he decided to keep praying anyway. In fact, he was so courageous that he didn't even try to hide his time of prayer.

> Now when Daniel knew that the document was signed, he entered his house (now in his roof chamber he had windows open toward Jerusalem); and he continued kneeling on his knees three times a day, praying and giving thanks before his God, as he had been doing previously (Daniel 6:10).

Daniel knew His God and was determined to stand strong in a godless culture. But he knew he could not do it on his own, so he turned to the Lord on behalf of his nation and prayed.

Naturally, the leaders betrayed Daniel to the king, and Darius was forced to send Daniel to the lions' den. But as he spoke the orders for his friend's death, Darius said, "Your God whom you constantly serve will Himself deliver you" (6:16). At least, the king hoped so.

Darius didn't eat or sleep that night, agonizing over having sent his friend to death. The drama is so good here, I will let you read for yourself what happened next:

> Very early the next morning he hurried out to the lions' den, and called out in anguish, "O Daniel, servant of the Living God, was your God, whom you worship continually, able to deliver you from the lions?"
> Then he heard a voice! "Your Majesty, live forever!" It was Daniel! "My God has sent his angel," he said, "to shut the lions' mouths so that they can't touch me; for I am innocent before God, nor, sir have I wronged you."
> The king was beside himself with joy and ordered that Daniel be lifted from the den. And not a scratch was found on him, because he believed in his God (6:19-23, LB).

We find out that Daniel's miraculous escape couldn't be blamed on friendly lions, because the evil leaders who got Daniel in trouble were then thrown into the den by King Darius. Before the men even reached the bottom of the pit, the lions overtook them and destroyed them.

What a phenomenal story of God's faithfulness in answer to this young man's faith and obedience. Not only did God protect him from death, but He used Daniel to change the heart of King Darius, a pagan, who turned from his ways and chose to honor God before the nation. Following Daniel's miracle in the den, the king wrote a new decree:

> I make a decree that in all the dominion of my kingdom men are to fear and tremble before the God of Daniel; for He is the living God and enduring forever, and His kingdom is one which will not be destroyed, and His dominion will be forever (6:26).

God is looking for people like Daniel today—young men and women who will stand as a testimony of righteousness and holiness. He's looking for someone who will choose to honor God at whatever expense, whether that means sacrificing reputation or even safety.

I love reading about young people in the Bible who answered that call from God. People like King Josiah, the praying teen-ager:

> Josiah was eight years old when he became king, and he reigned thirty-one years in Jerusalem. And he did right in the sight of the Lord, and walked in the ways of his father David and did not turn aside to the right or to the left. For in the eighth year of his reign while he was

still a youth, he began to seek the God of his father David; and in the twelfth year he began to purge Judah and Jerusalem of the high places, the Asherim, the carved images, and the molten images (2 Chronicles 34:1-3).

You can't tell it from this short passage, but Josiah's father and grandfather ranked as two of the most wicked kings in all of Israel's history. Yet God used this young teen-ager (at the age of 16) to turn an entire nation back to God. God was not limited by Josiah's ungodly upbringing or dysfunctional family. He recognized Josiah's heart—a heart that longed to serve Him—and that was all that God required.

I encourage you to study this fantastic story as well as the stories of many other young people called in the Bible to serve the Lord. You can read about David, a courageous shepherd boy; or Mary, the young girl chosen to be Jesus' mother. Paul wrote several letters to his young friend, Timothy, getting him ready for ministry. Esther wasn't very old when she risked her life to save the people of God, and young Samuel had to deliver some pretty uncomfortable news from God to the adult who was training him. Their stories remind me that age doesn't matter to God! Instead, like 2 Chronicles 16:9 says, "The eyes of the Lord move to and fro throughout the earth that He may strongly support those whose heart is completely His." God just wants people who've given themselves over to Him.

He sees the potential of youth today, and He obviously

hasn't stopped using them since these stories were recorded in the Bible. According to Dr. J. Edwin Orr, seven of nine major revivals in history began and were sustained by youth. America's history was even altered by a young man.[1] Samuel Mills, described as lanky in appearance and having a croaking voice, was known as someone dangerous to be around because he took the matter of prayer seriously! As a freshman at Williams Wood College, Samuel gathered five of his friends for a regular prayer meeting on Wednesday and Saturday afternoons in 1806. Because of opposition from other students on campus, the group met outside.

One day they were forced to take shelter under a haystack when a thunderstorm interrupted their time. They continued their prayer meeting under the haystack through the noise of the thunder and lightening. They had been studying Asia in their geography class at school, and became aware of the great need in Asia for the gospel of Jesus Christ.

As the students were praying for the evangelization of Asia, Samuel Mills said, "We can do it if we will! We ourselves can go!" This was quite a radical statement since no mission organizations existed in America at this time in history. One of the students objected, saying they'd all be killed, but Samuel Mills and the other students insisted that God wanted the advancement of His kingdom. They knew that if they did their part, their God could be counted on to do His. So with prayer and determination they dedicated their lives to help fulfill the

---

1 Timothy C. Wallstrom, *The Creation of a Student Movement to Evangelize the World* (Pasadena, CA: William Carey International University Press, 1980).

Great Commission. Samuel Mills prayed, "Lord, may the artillery of heaven be aimed against those who dare to lift one finger to oppose your heralds of the gospel around the world!"

Young Samuel's prayers marked the beginning of the Student Volunteer Movement, which literally sent more than 30,000 students into the mission field. Their slogan was, "The Evangelization of the World in This Generation," and, ignited through prayer, the movement resulted in a worldwide harvest that is still having an impact today. Oh, for this same spiritual fervor and dedication today among the youth of our nation! As the year 2000 approaches, let's rekindle this fire and allow God to use us as "fire seeds of spiritual awakening."

Let me explain this unusual phrase. Dr. Joon Gon Kim of Korea defines fire seeds as those people who bear the seed of the gospel and the fire of the Holy Spirit. "Fire seeds have no limitations. They can glow and grow and burn and blossom wherever they are planted. A fire seed cannot help but grow and multiply if he is equipped with the Gospel and the power of the Holy Spirit. It only takes a fire seed to ignite spiritual fires which in turn set the world aflame."[2]

As we commit ourselves to become fire seeds, we can capture our campuses and our nation for Christ. But I believe it begins with humility and prayer.

If My people, who are called by My name, will humble themselves and pray and seek My face and turn from their

---

2 Dan Hayes, *Fireseeds Of Spiritual Awakening* (San Bernardino, CA: Here's Life Publishers, Inc., 1983), p. 95.

wicked ways, then will I hear from heaven and will forgive their sin and will heal their land (2 Chronicles 7:14, NIV).

Beginning with prayer, great things will be accomplished: "Call to Me, and I will answer you, and I will tell you great and mighty things, which you do not know" (Jeremiah 33:3).

As Youth Congress '85 concluded and the students were leaving to go back to their high schools, I felt as if the Lord had given me a glimpse of what He wanted to do among the youth of our nation and world, particularly through the power of prayer. Four years later God began to put the vision before me and several other youth leaders with even more clarity. God, we sensed, wanted us to call students and youth leaders together to pray for our nation. We wanted them to understand that they could get on their knees and take a stand! We called it "Something's Happening USA," and on Labor Day weekend of 1989, we began what has since turned into an annual event. Approximately 1,000 high school students and leaders gathered from across the nation that year to pray. Only time and eternity will know the full impact from these meetings.

I am convinced the Lord desires our attention far more than we are willing to give it to Him. In His presence we are transformed into His likeness and made like vessels whom He can pour His life into. Of course, only God can accomplish His purposes. We are "receivers" of His grace and mercy, and then we can choose to become "reflectors" of His glory and goodness to our world.

Prayer is not something we do for God to please Him or some manipulation tool to get Him to act. It is an intimate relationship where first He hears us, then communicates with us, and finally fills us with more of Himself. What joy and power comes through this experience called prayer! In prayer we can truly be ourselves, expressing who God made us to be. There is really no special criteria for prayer except that we come before God with a clean heart: "If I regard wickedness in my heart, the Lord will not hear" (Psalm 66:18). He also demands that we address Him with a humble spirit:

> For thus says the High and Lofty One who inhabits eternity, whose name is Holy: "I dwell in the high and holy place, with him who has a contrite and humble spirit, to revive the spirit of the humble, and to revive the heart of the contrite ones" (Isaiah 57:15, NKJ).

Prayer opens up our eyes to see Him as He really is, and to see ourselves as desperately in need of Him. In spite of this difference, God remains passionately in love with us and desires our intimate communion with Him. As this truth has become so real to me, it's been a privilege to help begin a ministry called "Passionate Hearts: Women Desiring Intimacy with God." The greatest need in all of our lives is an intimate love relationship with the God who created us. As we grow in our understanding of this, we respond in gratitude and expectation of how He has provided prayer as the key to His heart.

What an incredible privilege it is to come before our King and lay our needs, desires and burdens before Him. He alone can unlock whatever barrier we may feel and don't understand. He will then show us what steps to take for further repentance, healing or obedience. As we listen and respond to Him, our intimacy with Him really can have an impact on the world! The world is not in need of perfect people, but it is in need of people who have been touched by the saving, healing grace that Jesus offers. When they see that in us and learn that this is available to them, our intimacy with God affects those around us. Besides, in prayer God gives us our marching orders and the power to carry those orders out.

Out of a desire to have a spiritual impact at their high school, one group of students from Lake Brantley High School in Orlando formed a Prayer Force on their campus. They became part of a movement of students seeking God earnestly for their peers, family, community and nation. A junior named Mike described their early morning prayer meetings as the "Command Center" where they sought the will of their Heavenly Captain.

Through prayer, God creatively led these students to host a Valentine's Day outreach. They ordered 800 flowers to give out to all the girls in the school. Along with the flowers, the students passed out invitations to an evangelistic Valentine's Day party. The students believed God would draw a large crowd, so they raised money for pizza and a band. God overcame all barriers, and they were even able to have the event in their school auditorium. They put together a terrific program, including funny skits and several personal testimonies about how some of them first met Jesus and became Christians. The evening concluded with an invitation for people to pray and receive Jesus' unconditional love.

God answered my friends' prayers abundantly. That night, 40 students received Christ. How incredible it is to realize that we are partners with the Lord through prayer! Maybe you need to alter your perspective on prayer. Remember, prayer does not prepare us for the work; prayer *is* the work! As we learn to seek Him in prayer, God gives us His directions and plan. All we have to do is step out in faith and obey.

Jesus Himself modeled a complete dependency upon His Father through prayer. In the pages of the Bible, we read about Jesus praying early in the morning while it is still dark, or sometimes praying all night before performing great miracles. His disciples observed this and recognized how different Jesus' understanding of prayer was from their understanding, so one day they asked Him to teach them how to pray.

Jesus's answer came through a simple yet profound example that we now call "The Lord's Prayer."

When you pray, say: 'Father, hallowed be Thy name. Thy kingdom come. Give us each day our daily bread.

And forgive us our sins, For we ourselves also forgive everyone who is indebted to us. And lead us not into temptation (Luke 11:2-4).

I think it will be worth stopping for a few minutes to analyze these words that many of us take for granted.

When Jesus told His disciples to address their prayers to "Our Father," He reminded them that they belonged to Him and that they were His precious children. We have so many reasons to offer God our *thanksgiving*; among them is our position of being His child.

Second, Jesus' example reminded them that God's name was "hallowed" or "holy." Jesus wanted His disciples to understand that God demands our *adoration*. He is the God who rules the universe, and He deserves our submission.

When Jesus told His disciples to ask for daily bread, He was encouraging them to boldly ask for every need. Another word for that is *supplication*.

And finally, Jesus taught His disciples about the importance of prayers of *confession* when He included forgiveness in His lesson. When we confess our sins and shortcomings to God with a humble heart, He promises to forgive us and even strengthen us against further temptation.

These four parts—thanksgiving, adoration, supplication and confession—can be rearranged into an acronym for easy recall: ACTS. As we learn to express our ACTS (adoration, confession, thanksgiving and supplication) of prayer to God, we can have confidence in God's desire to answer us. His answer may not look exactly the way we expected or hoped, but we can be sure He will answer.

I had the privilege of having a praying mom who taught me so much about communication with God. While I was growing up, she prayed that one of her six children would have a "vocation" or calling to serve God full-time. In her mind, she thought that call would be as a nun. God definitely heard her prayers, but He answered in a different way than she expected. At first, she resisted God's answer, but through prayer and the surrender of her own heart to Jesus, she has since embraced His plan for me, her daughter. My mom continues to be my number one prayer partner and a role model of prayer.

Even as a little girl, Mom taught me that I could pray to God as my Heavenly Father, and she said I could tell Him anything. I didn't yet fully understand a personal relationship with Jesus, but my precious mother gave me a hunger to communicate with God.

I'd like to invite you to enter into this kind of partnership with God through prayer. God is creative, so try different ways to spend time with Him in prayer. Let Him lead you in the adventure. Remember the four parts of prayer that we learned from Jesus' example (ACTS). If you are feeling stuck, begin by asking yourself the following questions, and maybe set a few goals:

- How can I improve my personal prayer life? Do I need a daily prayer journal? How about choosing a time and place to pray?

- Is there a group or person at my school, office or neighborhood that I could pray with?
- Could God use me to be a "fire seed" for calling others to pray? Maybe He would want me to form a Prayer Force on my campus or in my community, see *Active in the Mission*, p.190.

Let me tell you about a simple prayer strategy called "prayer triplets" that many students and adults across the nation are using. It involves three friends committing to pray together regularly for:

1) each other's daily walk with God;
2) the salvation of nine friends (three names per person);
3) spiritual awakening in the group's campus, nation and world.

As you develop your prayer life, God can use you to be an agent for awakening on your campus, in your community, nation and throughout your world. You will be a part of the largest prayer movement in history. Missionary statesman Ralph Winter said, "We have before us the brightest set of hope-filled resources, the most extensive global network of global believers in prayer and strategy."[3]

We have never had as many competent, sold-out soldiers for Jesus Christ. We are a part of the army of the Living God, and our çaptain is the Lord of Hosts. We know He will be

3 David Bryant, *Hope at Hand* (Grand Rapids, MI: Baker Book House, 1995), p.221.

victorious, and we can be a part of bringing forth His victory.

God wants to inflame you with a fresh passion for Himself, a passion He will use to change your generation. He wants to use you to make a difference, and all He asks is that you listen for His orders. Simply put—pray, then obey.

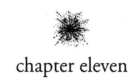

chapter eleven

Look among the nations! Observe! Be astonished! Wonder!
Because I am doing something in your days—You would not
believe if you were told.

Habakkuk 1:5

Mission: Possible

I was alone in the desert, surrounded by sand, rock and cactus. And I was glad.

"Canaan in the Desert" in Phoenix, Arizona, has become my favorite retreat spot, and I had begun to make it a tradition of mine to spend time there. Out in the desert I can seek God about direction for my future without many distractions, and there I bask in His love and sacrifice for me.

This particular time, I ventured out early in the morning to hike up a nearby mountain. Climbing through the rocks and rugged terrain made me think of the Lord Jesus and the 40 days He spent in the desert preparing for His mission. I came across

Mission Road, and just because the name seemed so appropriate to my reason for being out there, I decided to follow it. When I got to the end of Mission Road, I ventured out into the desert, trying to make my own path up the mountain overlooking the desert. Without a clear-cut path, however, it was not quite as easy as I first anticipated. But this was the kind of adventure I loved, charting my own course and making a way where it didn't seem possible.

The Holy Spirit reminded me that this was what my adventure of faith is all about. Being led by the Holy Spirit, step by step; walking by faith, not by sight. I repeated a little made-up rhyme in my mind on that journey as I prayed, "Lead me on to greater heights, fixed on purely heavenly sights."

I kept walking, growing tired, but all the while rejoicing at the insights that God was giving me. The desert itself is usually a symbol of barrenness, yet God had been speaking to me out in this dry land about the new work He was doing in my life. I reflected on the 23 years that He had allowed me to be in full-time Christian ministry. Like my hike in the desert, much of that path had been unclear at the time. I could only keep looking up with my eyes fixed on Jesus, my goal and my final destination.

I also had discovered how to rely on the Holy Spirit's guidance, knowing He would lead me on the path that was charted just for me. I never would have dreamed that 25 years after giving my heart to Jesus, He would have led me to more than 30 countries in the world sharing His great love and forgiveness. How could I have known that God would grant me the privilege of helping to provide leadership to youth and youth leaders around the world? Little did I know that my decision to become a Christian would make me God's simple servant, entrusted to help mobilize prayer for our nation. Recently He has led me to help launch Passionate Hearts, a retreat ministry for women desiring intimacy with God. And I know there is more He has in store, things which I cannot imagine. Only the Father knows the course that I will take, because only the Father knows the future. One of my favorite Christian authors, Corrie Ten Boom, wrote: "No need to worry about the future. God is already there!"

As I arrived at the top of the mountain that night in Phoenix, I watched the sun go down softly, creating one of the most incredible sunsets I have ever seen. All was still and peaceful. Again, I couldn't help but think about the intimate times Jesus spent in the wilderness with His Father. And He had come to show us the way to the Father. Through our love relationship with Jesus, we can begin to know our Heavenly Father the way Jesus did. As we also embrace the mission which the Father has laid out for us, we will experience an intimate partnership with Him.

The sky grew darker as I was up on the mountain, but the light in my heart grew brighter. The stars began to sparkle, and God's glory was shining all around me. Shortly after my sunset experience, I took out my journal and wrote a poem expressing some of these thoughts:

Creator, Master, Lover of my soul,
Great I AM, You made me whole.
The heavens declare Your glory
revealing Your eternal story.
You called the stars by name;
Brilliant clouds radiate your fame.
Yet the wonder up above
cannot describe Your tender love.
Oh, that my lips could recite
More of You and Your might!
Words could not begin to recount
Love so amazing, endless Fount.
My beloved, You are mine.
This treasure, joy divine,
I give you my life, my all,
with gratefulness for Your call.
With adoration I bow and wait
for You to meet me at the Gate.

Indeed our life is a mission that will be concluded one day when we meet Him face-to-face. Until then, He has a path, a mission, for each one of us that is charted ahead of time. All we must do is take His hand and walk with Him on this exciting journey, this adventure of faith. He promises, "I will instruct you and teach you in the way which you should go; I will counsel you with My eye upon you" (Psalm 32:8).

Christopher Columbus knew the adventure of faith. Unfortunately, many of our history books leave his faith, a central part of Columbus' drive, out of the picture. They don't tell the whole story.

Within the pages of his own personal journals, we learn much more about this courageous young man. Christopher, which literally means Christ-bearer, was convinced God had given him a special mission: to carry the Light of Christ into the darkness of undiscovered, heathen lands. His call was to introduce the inhabitants of these lands to the holy faith of Christianity. Throughout his journal he quoted lines of Scripture from the book of Isaiah, which must have confirmed his call:

> Listen, O isles, unto me; and hearken, ye people, from far; The Lord hath called me from the womb; from the bowels of my mother hath He made mention of my name . . . . and He said . . . "I will also give thee for a light to the Gentiles, that thou mayest be my salvation unto the end of the earth" (Isaiah 49:1,6b, KJV).

No one knows for sure when his sense of mission crystallized; it very well could have begun as a teenage boy. Columbus himself writes this:

It was the Lord who put into my mind (I could feel His hand upon me) the fact that it would be possible to sail from here to the Indies. All who heard of my project rejected it with laughter, ridiculing me. There is no question that the inspiration was from the Holy Spirit, because He comforted me with rays of marvelous inspiration from the Holy Scriptures. . . . For the execution of the journey to the Indies, I did not make use of intelligence, mathematics or maps. It is simply the fulfillment of what Isaiah had prophesied. . . . No one should fear to undertake any task in the name of our Savior, if it is just and if the intention is purely for His holy service. The working out of all things has been assigned to each person by our Lord, but it all happens according to His sovereign will, even though He gives advice. He lacks nothing that it is in the power of men to give Him. Oh, what a gracious Lord, who desires that people should perform for Him those things for which He holds Himself responsible![1]

What a testimony of Columbus' complete dependence upon the Lord in this divine enterprise. I've often thought about how his obedience to follow the Holy Spirit has had a huge impact on our nation's history and consequently on the entire world. Like Columbus wrote, God has a divine destiny for nations, but He also holds one for individuals. We dare not

---

1 Peter Marshall and David Manuel, *The Light and the Glory* (Old Tappan, N.J.: Fleming H. Revell Company, 1977), p. 17.

forfeit our high and holy calling as a nation through personal lives of neglect and sin.

Throughout history, God has called individuals to be instruments for His divine purposes. What a privilege to be in partnership with God! There are many examples in the Bible of people both young and old who have been called by God to a divine task or vocation. The word *call* is very common in both the Old Testament and the New Testament, with over 700 instances of its use.

Samuel, for instance, was called by God as a young man. In the book of 1 Samuel, we can read about God's call to Samuel. Late at night, after everyone had gone to sleep, young Samuel woke up and actually heard someone call his name. He figured it was the voice of Eli, the priest whom Samuel lived with. At first, Eli was confused too, but then the priest discerned that Samuel was probably hearing the call of God.

> And Eli said to Samuel, "Go lie down, and it shall be if He calls you, that you shall say, 'Speak Lord, for Thy servant is listening.'" So Samuel went and lay down in his place. Then the Lord came and stood and called as at other times, "Samuel! Samuel!" And Samuel said, "Speak, for Thy servant is listening" (1 Samuel 3:9,10).

Samuel responded in an attitude of obedience. The story continues with Samuel getting a message from God which He wanted the boy to pass on. Samuel was called to play a crucial role as God's spokesman.

Mary is an example of a young teenage girl who received a call from God. According to the first chapter of Luke, an angel appeared out of nowhere, and greeted young Mary with these words: "Hail, favored one! The Lord is with you." The Bible tells us that the angels' words troubled her. How would you feel if an angel appeared to you out of the blue? "And the angel said to her, 'Do not be afraid, Mary, for you have found favor with God'" (Luke 1:30).

Not a typical day in Mary's life! After the angel tried to reassure her that everything was OK, he told Mary that she would be used in God's eternal plan to bring the promised Messiah into the world. Mary's response was so beautiful. From those words alone, I can see why God chose her: "And Mary said, 'Behold the bondslave of the Lord; be it done to me according to your word'" (Luke 1:38). Mary had already learned to trust God. She knew He was faithful to His Word. God knew He could entrust her with His Son because this young woman already had a heart committed to Him.

Are you learning to obey and trust Him as you walk with Him each day? Is His Word becoming more real to you? Do you hide it in your heart? Can you hear His voice when He calls?

I've been challenged as I've read biographies of ordinary men and women used by God to build His kingdom. Amy Carmichael is one such woman. She came to know the Lord at

13 years old, and at 17 she sensed God's call on her life. She threw herself into His service, starting a schoolgirl's prayer meeting. She volunteered at the YWCA, held children's Bible meetings, taught night school in slums and organized a morning watch of prayer and Bible reading.

Little did she know that God was preparing her to become a missionary to India. God used Amy's life (from 1867-1951) to make a profound Christian impact in India. Beyond that, He also used her powerfully in the lives of those who have read her books and journals. Amy expressed a deep devotion and spiritual commitment to Jesus in those pages, and as one of her readers, I was challenged just by reading about her call and her courageous faith to obey.

One of the most astonishing stories I've read is *Bruchko*. It's the story of a 19-year-old's adventures in teaching the Motilone tribe about Jesus. But before he became an evangelist to the murderous South American tribe, Bruce Olson struggled in high school with the question, "Who is my God?" He'd been raised by a church-going family, and even knew the theology of his church. But Bruce wanted to know God personally.

His search led him into the Bible, and at 2 a.m. one night, he asked Jesus to change him and to make him new. The Lord knew his heart's cry, and He led Bruce to a personal faith in Jesus Christ. From that point on, Bruce couldn't keep it to himself. He wrote in his book, "I've got to share this . . . It will change my family completely. And the kids at church. They need to know Jesus, too."

Bruce faced conflict and misunderstanding in his family and among some of his peers, because he so desperately wanted them to know Christ. But he determined to be a witness for Christ in his high school, and to follow God's plan for his life. All the while God was strengthening and preparing him for his future call as a missionary.

I've witnessed something like this in the lives of many young men and women. I smile when I think of my friend Keith. As a teen-ager, he just had a natural personality for gathering people. Keith spent his freshman year at parties and influenced many to join him. Then God brought Keith to faith in Jesus. After this dramatic change, he started bringing all his friends to hear about Jesus, and he began to personally share his faith.

I loved to sit down and hear what God was teaching Keith. One day at a McDonald's restaurant, Keith leaned across the table and told me about the call he thought God had given him. "Nancy," he said, "I am praying about China. Think of all the people there who need to hear the gospel." I was a bit surprised that, as a young Christian, Keith's burden passed the borders of his country and into uncharted territory. So I encouraged him to keep praying and asked God to nurture that seed in his heart.

On the night many Chinese students were massacred in Tiananmen Square, I sat glued to my television set, wondering and praying about Keith. Yes, God had faithfully fulfilled the vision Keith told me about in McDonald's several years before. Keith was now serving Christ in China. When he returned from China for a brief sabbatical, I asked him, "Where were you that night?" Keith recounted the stories of several of his young disciples who had shared their faith with the soldiers in the square and were later killed. Today, God is continuing to use Keith to minister to Chinese leaders.

Who knows what special purpose God has for your life? Will you respond with eagerness and anticipation to the Lord's call? It is individuals like you and me whom God has chosen to change the course of this generation. Thankfully, those who have lived before us have answered God's call and carried His message to a world in need of hearing it. Because of their faithfulness, you and I have a rich spiritual heritage. Like a runner passing a baton in a marathon, the apostle Paul challenged young Timothy in the Bible, asking him to continue carrying the truths of Jesus: "And the things which you have heard from me in the presence of many witnesses, these entrust to faithful men, who will be able to teach others also" (2 Timothy 2:2).

Paul is one of my favorite heroes of the Christian faith. He was indeed a man chosen with a mission, and he recognized his partnership with Jesus Christ. Paul lived in radical abandonment to Jesus Christ, and we are the recipients. Following his example, many continue to carry the gospel to others.

Paul knew young Timothy might be intimidated by this duty because of his age, but he wanted him to know that God would use him as a model for others. We see proof of that in his advice: "Let no one look down on your youthfulness, but rather in speech, conduct, love, faith and purity, show yourself an example of those who believe" (1 Timothy 4:12). Just before he died, Paul left Timothy this charge:

> Preach the word; be ready in season and out of season; reprove, rebuke, exhort, with great patience and instruction. For the time will come when they will not endure sound doctrine. . . (2 Timothy 4:2,3).

I dare you to take up this charge for yourself. Make God's mission your mission, and embrace your destiny. Only He knows the adventure in faith that lies ahead for you. As you recognize your calling as an ambassador for Jesus Christ, I don't know where that call will lead you, but I can promise you that God has incredible things in store for you. The world is watching and waiting for people who will abandon themselves completely to Jesus Christ. William Carey, a pioneer missionary to India, exhorted Christians this way: "Expect great things *from* God; attempt great things *for* God."

Start today and ask God what mission He has for you to fulfill. What step of faith is He asking you to take? Are you willing to venture beyond the borders of your country for a short-term mission trip? Begin to pray for the world, asking your Heavenly Father what part you can play in helping to fulfill

His Great Commission.

Are you preparing yourself in the meantime by being an example of purity, love and commitment to Jesus Christ? Are you exercising your gifts and talents and seeking to invest them in God's kingdom? You may want to get some counsel from someone who knows you and can help you to do this.

Look for someone like the apostle Paul in your life, a person of the same sex who can help mentor you spiritually and lead you along in your spiritual walk. Don't hesitate to seek out someone at church whom you admire and would like to learn from. If you can't think of anyone, ask God to bring someone into your life.

Next, begin to keep a journal of the dreams and desires that God begins to lay on your heart. Finally, seek God's will above your own. Ask God to reveal the divine purpose He has for you, and submit yourself to His plan. Become a revolutionary in your generation—accept the Mission: Possible!

In the song "The Mission," Steve Green sings about that mission which God calls us to in His Word:

There's a call going out across the land in every nation,
A call to all who swear allegiance to the cross of Christ;
A call to true humility, to live our lives responsibly;
To deepen our devotion to the Cross at any price.
Let us then be sober moving only in the Spirit,
As aliens and strangers in a hostile and foreign land;

The message we're proclaiming is repentance
and forgiveness—
The offer of salvation to the dying race of man.
To love the Lord our God is the heartbeat of our mission,
The spring from which our service overflows.
Across the street or around the world, the mission's still
the same:
Proclaim and live the Truth, in Jesus' name!

Just remember, there is an urgency to this mission. God has called us to reach a dying world. Half of the world's population has never heard the name of Jesus—thousands are plunging daily into hell. The next chapter addresses this sense of urgency through the eyes of a young woman facing her own time-sensitive mission.

chapter twelve

. . . and if I perish, I perish.

Esther 4:16l

For Such a Time as This

I can still remember sitting in church, 12 years old, making a vow to God: "I promise that I will go to be a missionary in Africa. If I don't go, You can kill me."

Many years later (I was not dead yet) an opportunity was calling me to Africa. I heard that still, small voice whisper in my heart, *Now is the time to go to Africa. The doors are opening up as never before.* The event was called Love Southern Africa, a conference held in Johannesburg that would equip and train 5,000 people and send them out as short-term missionaries into various parts of the continent. I joined 40 American adults and teen-agers who accepted the challenge to go. We were sent to

Swaziland and divided into five teams to help saturate the country with the gospel. Our teams were mixed of all cultures and countries, a small example of how God was uniting His body to fulfill His purpose through this outreach.

After much prayer, God opened the door for our teams to make presentations at public-school assemblies. The students and I also shared our faith in our teams, visiting hospitals and huts. We even set up a microphone at the huge train station in the capital city.

On one particular afternoon, we had been in the city meeting people and sharing the love of Christ with them. We finally sat to have lunch at Kentucky Fried Chicken. (Believe it or not, the "Colonel" is all over the world!) After I finished eating, I noticed a beautiful young woman, and I introduced myself. Her name was Angel. As I got to know her, she told me she was married to a prince. It surprised me to think that royalty would eat at Kentucky Fried Chicken.

Knowing the culture, I understood that princes often have several wives. So I asked her, "Does your husband have more than one wife?"

"Oh no, only me," Angel replied.

"Does he have other girlfriends?" I asked with curiosity.

"No," she responded, "right now he's being very good." Then Angel asked me if I was married. In the African culture, being a single woman is not looked upon so keenly, and Angel looked sad for me when I told her that I was not married.

"Nancy," she asked, "if my husband came to meet you, and asked you to marry him, would you? I could ask my husband to come and meet you, and he could ask you to marry him." I was shocked and had to laugh aloud at the offer. Not many women have offered their husbands to me before.

"Thanks," I answered, "but no thanks. Even though I don't have an earthly husband, I do have a Royal Prince to whom I belong. Would you mind if I told you about Him?"

Naturally, Angel was very curious. That day I had the royal privilege of introducing her to the King of kings.

It is true, we all have a Royal Prince and have direct access to the King of kings. That royal access is a position which God has given us for a reason, as He did in the Bible with Queen Esther. Her story has always been fascinating to me, but even more so recently as I have pondered and prayed over the needs of our generation. Let me retell Esther's inspiring story for you and show you how it portrays the royal position with which God endowed her for the sake of a nation.

Esther was a young Jewish girl living in Susa, the capital city of ancient Persia. She was an orphan brought up by her uncle Mordecai, but her claim to fame was great beauty. People were charmed and fascinated by it, including the king, once he discovered her.

Long before he had ever seen her, King Xerxes decided that he wanted a new queen. His servants arranged a beauty pageant where the grand prize was not a scholarship or a new wardrobe, but the king himself, and all that came with being his bride. Beautiful virgins were brought from all over the land to the king's palace where they were treated to a 12-month makeover, complete with spices, cosmetics and perfumes. One ordinary day in Esther's life turned out to change her entire future, when the king's caravan came through her city gathering the most beautiful young virgins. Esther was taken (apparently against her will) to the king's palace for this massive beauty contest.

Put yourself in Esther's shoes for a moment. Imagine how frightened the young teen-age girl probably felt, whisked away from her family and from everything familiar. Esther had no choice but to trust in her God. As the drama proceeds, Esther captivates the king with her beauty and was chosen by him to be his queen.

Her new regal position opens up an entirely new dimension to her life, and to the life of the Jewish people. She now shared the throne with the king through a special partnership. But Esther did not yet know why, in God's sovereignty, that she was transformed into royalty.

As the story continues to unfold, we learn of a plot by an evil man named Haman who wants to destroy the Jewish people. He proposes his scheme to the king, who in turn approves the plan and passes an edict. Suddenly, Esther's life takes on tremendous significance. She had to tell the king that his edict would wipe out her people, but that required approaching the king in his inner court without first being summoned. Queen

Esther knew that anyone—even his wife—who did this faced certain death (Esther 4:11). So now she faced the biggest decision of her life: Would she risk her life on behalf of her people, the Jews? Her uncle, Mordecai, coached her with wise counsel:

> Do not imagine that you in the king's palace can escape any more than all the Jews. For if you remain silent at this time, relief and deliverance will arrive for the Jews from another place and you and your father's house will perish. And who knows whether you have not attained royalty for such a time as this? (Esther 4:13,14).

God had been preparing Esther for this one divine moment. She had learned to trust Mordecai's leadership, knowing God often worked through him. Her faith in God had been groomed by obedience. So when her convictions were tested, Queen Esther chose to put her life on the line and go before the king on behalf of her nation. Much to her relief, she obtained special favor from the king during her visit in his inner court, as seen when he extended his golden scepter to her and said, "What is your petition, Queen Esther? It shall be granted you. And what is your request? Even to half of the kingdom it shall be done" (Esther 7:2b).

Esther pleaded for her people, and through her influence, her nation was spared. Esther indeed was a heroine, one chosen for a critical moment in history! As I meditate on her life, I see how we, too, have been chosen at a critical hour in history. But first, let's re-examine her situation.

What specifically made Esther a heroine, and how can we learn from her example? First of all, she faced the problem of her generation head-on. She was in great distress over the plight of her people and cared enough to get involved. I imagine she could have just ignored the decree that jeopardized the Jews, somehow hoping that at least she would be safe as queen. But she didn't.

Second, she knew her position. Through the advice of Mordecai, Esther recognized her unique role, one that she had been sovereignly placed in for that moment in history. If anyone had the power to change the king's mind, certainly it would have to be his queen. Third, she tapped into the king's power. She decided to go to the king, regardless of the consequences. She was willing to pay the price. Her famous words, "If I perish, I perish," from Esther 4:16 demonstrate her courageous commitment to the cause.

Just as Esther rose to fulfill her mission, so we too can rise to meet the challenge of our generation—to lead them to a personal relationship with Jesus Christ. As we recognize the needs of our generation and begin to care deeply for those needs, God will give us His heart of compassion and concern. Esther knew her royal position and had special access to the king; we are also clothed with the righteousness of Christ and have obtained the King's favor. He is delighted with us and wants to share His riches with us. I can envision Him holding out His royal scepter to us saying, "What is your request? I want to share my blessings and power with you."

This story became so personal to me as I contemplated the truth of my position in Christ as His bride and thought more about the partnership that He shares with me now and for all eternity! What an awesome privilege! However, with that partnership and position comes an urgency. Indeed, it seems our world is on a collision course with disaster, and we could be nearing the end of the age. America—our nation—is at a crossroads, where the foundations are being shaken to the core. We need godly young men and women willing to accept their royal position as Esther did.

We, like Esther, can be courageous, act on our convictions and turn to the Lord for help. Esther used her royal position to respond to her royal responsibility. Courageously, she formulated her plan, even if it meant dying in the effort. She fasted and called others to join her for three days and nights—a display of humility and utter dependence upon God's sovereign intervention. Esther fought for her nation, those who had been condemned. And God used Esther to spare them.

I believe that our compassionate Father is waiting for those of us who love Him to pray for those who don't yet know Him. Unless they know Jesus, they also have been given a decree of death, like Esther's people were condemned.

In the blockbuster movie *Titanic* we see a modern example of urgency ignored. The night after I saw it, I woke up sweating from a nightmare, with vivid pictures from the movie replaying in my mind. I could still see all those people, falling, falling,

falling; hundreds of them screaming as they dropped into the frigid waters of the ocean.

How ironic that the largest, most luxurious ship of its day, the one that represented man's greatest achievements—a ship about which men boasted, "God Himself could not sink this ship"—might become a graveyard for 1,500 people. Out of 2,340 passengers aboard, only 840 survived.

The captain and his crew were radioed from off the ship, alerting the crew with seven warnings about iceberg danger, but the warnings were ignored. Once the ship was struck, the passengers would not believe that the ship was sinking. Some even refused to get into the lifeboats, worrying their clothes might wrinkle. They continued partying and drinking, even throwing snowball fights with chunks from the same iceberg that ripped open the ship's hull.

I see a similarity to our culture today. People won't acknowledge the dangerous moral erosion around the world, blissfully ignoring the fact that many are plunging to an eternity without Jesus Christ. We have a different Captain, One who knows the condition of our world in crisis. He has given a clarion call to join Him in rescuing our generation from the disaster of an eternal destiny without Him. He has entrusted us with His Great Commission.

We can be used by God at this hour of history to issue a rescue call to those facing eternal danger. Will you be a lifesaver for this generation? We are here on this earth for one reason, and that is to complete the purpose that Jesus came for—"to seek and to save that which was lost" (Luke 19:10). Together, let's fulfill the words that were said of Him in Isaiah 61:

> The Spirit of the Sovereign Lord is on me, because the Lord has anointed me to preach good news to the poor. He has sent me to bind up the brokenhearted, to proclaim freedom for the captives and release from darkness for the prisoners, to proclaim the year of the Lord's favor and the vengeance of our God, to comfort all who mourn (Isaiah 61:1,2, NIV).

At this time, people are open to the gospel like never before. Between now and the year 2025, 3.2 billion people will be added to the world's population. Ninety-five percent of those will be in poor countries. We know that Jesus is the answer people need and seek.

I'm praying "that you may become blameless and pure, children of God without fault in a crooked and depraved generation, in which you shine like stars in the universe as you hold out the word of life . . ." (Philippians 2:15,16b, NIV).

This truly is the hour of destiny for Christians to shine as beacon lights. Many believe that we are facing the final frontiers of world missions. There is a growing sense that the Great Commission is coming to completion, and this could very well be the generation that sees it fulfilled.

But let's not stop so long to wonder at the mighty acts of God and meanwhile miss the urgency of reaping that harvest. Jesus said, "As long as it is day, we must do the work of Him who sent Me. Night is coming, when no one can work" (John 9:4, NIV).

That sense of urgency requires a passionate response from us. In his book, *Passion for Jesus,* Mike Bickle addresses this need for passion. He writes,

> Seeing the heart, mind, and character of God will cure our compromise and instability and motivate us to righteousness and holy passion. Personal, experiential knowledge of the person of Jesus will fuel obedience and zeal. It will put a stop to our restlessness and discontent. A new depth of intimacy with Him will extinguish our boredom and capture our hearts.[1]

The world is waiting for a generation which is intimately acquainted with Jesus. I believe God is raising up a generation of those who seek Him. Consider with me the challenge to take up your royal position as His bride before Almighty God, and boldly ask Him to use you. Ask Him for mercy for those destined for hell. Ask Him to send them new hearts, hearts that will hear and respond to the words of life. And ask Him for the nations, for he promises, "Ask of Me, and I will surely give the nations as Thine inheritance" (Psalm 2:8a). Our King is waiting for us to come to Him for such a time as this. We dare not wait.

1 Mike Bickle, *Passion for Jesus* (Lake Mary, FL: Creation House, 1993, p. 54). Used by permission.

Conclusion

Pivotal Generation

As I followed the Lord's leading in writing this book, I struggled with a sense of inadequacy. "Who am I to write a book?" I prayed. "And besides, Lord, I don't have any time!" Well, it took seven years for God to fully write the message in my heart and mind. He continued to nudge me along through the prayers and encouragement of others, and most often through His powerful Word. One night as I was praying, my Heavenly Father led me to read the words of Jeremiah:

Now the word of the Lord came to me saying, "Before I formed you in the womb I knew you, and before you were born I consecrated you; I have appointed you a prophet to the nations." Then I said, "Alas, Lord God! Behold, I do not know how to speak, because I am a youth." But the Lord said to me, "Do not say, 'I am a youth,' because everywhere I send you, you shall go, and all that I command you, you shall speak. Do not be afraid of them, for I am with you to deliver you," declares the Lord. Then the Lord stretched out His hand and touched my mouth, and the Lord said to me, "Behold, I have put My words in your mouth. See, I have appointed you this day over the nations and over the kingdoms. To pluck up and to break down, to destroy and to overthrow, to build and to plant" (Jeremiah 1:4-10).

I could identify with Jeremiah's fears expressed in this passage. Yet the reassuring words of the Lord dealt with every barrier I faced in writing my book. Like He told young Jeremiah, God only asks us to be willing and available. He promises to give us His words and power as He leads us in His plan.

Whatever barriers you may face as you attempt to recognize and follow God's plan for your life, I urge you to remember the source of that plan. Our great God is calling you, and He is looking for a righteous generation to which He can reveal Himself and His mission.

We can be like David, who "had served the purpose of God in his own generation" (Acts 13:36). We can be like the great men and women who have gone before us and claimed this promise:

Praise the Lord! How blessed is the man who fears the Lord, who greatly delights in His commandments. His descendants will be mighty on earth; the generation of the upright will be blessed (Psalm 112:1,2).

Could we be a pivotal generation in God's time line of history? Will our obedience to His Great Commission be the determining factor in bringing about His eternal Kingdom? "And the Good News about the Kingdom will be preached throughout the whole world, so that all nations will hear it; and then, finally the end will come" (Matthew 24:14, LB).

Hidden away in an old book called *Missionary Review of the World*, written in 1888, I found an article titled "The Supreme Questions of the Hour" by A.T. Pierson. The 100-year-old challenge that Pierson gave his readers also applies to us in this hour of history:

Has God a plan in this generation? If so, what is it, and how am I to know it? By every sign and signal God has shown the men of this generation that His purpose is the immediate evangelization of the world. The profit of such a business as winning souls, who can estimate it? There is another capital to invest besides the capital of money. Brains as well as brawn, mind and morals, gifts and graces, time and talents, acquisitions and accomplishments, the inherited and gathered riches of human character—knowledge, love, speech, life. Tell us, young man, young woman, you who wish to serve your own generation by the will of God, where will you find such opportunity for the investment of your intellectual, moral and spiritual capital? Do you want to make your life tell for God and man? Do you want to multiply yourself a thousand-fold, to make your tongue and your pen a redeeming factor in human history? Here is your chance.

Does that challenge resonate within your heart?

Let me tell you one last story about a man that I met who lived up to this challenge. We met in an art museum in Hungary, back in 1986. Communism still ruled the country. Along with 26 teen-agers and youth leaders, my whole mission group hid our Bibles and prayed our way past the Hungarian guards' checkpoints. Inside the country's borders, we asked the Lord to give us His divine appointments.

"God bless you," I whispered in Hungarian to the ticket-taker at the museum entrance. His crystal blue eyes pierced right through me and he smiled back, then quickly hugged me and kissed me on my cheeks. He whispered in return, "My sister, you must meet me tomorrow at the restaurant next door."

This was the last day of my trip, but I had a sense from God that this was a very important meeting. So I met this dear 74-year-old man, and he captivated me as he unfolded his story. For more than thirty years Uncle Francis, as he was affectionately known, served Jesus Christ as a missionary throughout Russia.

Taken captive by Communist soldiers, he had been sent to Siberian prison camps. He recalled marching through the frozen land, barely surviving.

The Lord spared his life, despite the fact that his brother and father both died in the camps. After three days of a very severe illness, he told me that he had been declared dead. But through a dream, he heard the voice of the Lord tell him that he would survive. Uncle Francis was told in his dream that God had a purpose for him that he had yet to fulfill.

Even when he described his sufferings, the old man's face glowed. He considered his life's experiences a privilege because he had been allowed to serve the One he called the "Great Slave." Jesus, he reminded me, was the greatest among servants.

Uncle Francis led many fellow prisoners to Jesus Christ. Inevitably, he was finally taken away to be shot, but he told the guards that he was so happy for the privilege to die for Jesus. The guards had enough of this godly man (or perhaps the Holy Spirit convicted them), so they released this fool for Christ instead of shooting him. He recounted this story's end with sadness, because he had been denied the privilege of dying in the name of His Savior.

Uncle Francis and I became dear friends and have corresponded through these years. I have many pages of letters from him, telling stories and testimonies of God's faithfulness. He usually ended his letters with a little symbol in Russian that translates into, "Jesus Christ is calling you!" Uncle Francis said he first heard the call when he was six years old, when his Sunday school teacher talked about being a missionary in Africa. He desperately wanted to go there because he heard that many people were being killed for Christ. "But God," he said, "had other plans." He sent me this poem that he had written:

I wanted to go South—He sent me East.
I wanted as soon as possible to die for Him in Africa—
He presented me a long life with suffering, experiences
and blessings in Europe and Asia.
I asked from Him one people—He gave me the whole manhood.
I asked from Him for "one"—He gave me "thousands!"
"Great and marvelous are Thy works,
O Lord God, the Almighty.
Righteous and true are Thy ways,
Thy King of the nations."

Like his poem suggests, God did not lead Uncle Francis to Africa, but instead allowed him to learn seven Slavic languages and travel to many parts of Europe and Asia. To this day, he is still proclaiming the gospel. Since the fall of Communism, religious freedom has again postponed his chance to die for Jesus' name. God clearly chose Uncle Francis for a mission. I am honored to call Uncle Francis one of my precious spiritual mentors and was able to celebrate his 80th birthday with him back in Hungary after communism had fallen.

In my own life, I can remember so vividly when I heard that clear call. God indeed had a purpose for me. Understanding that call was actually part of a longer process, but at one point in time, I began to evaluate my life: *How could I invest my life in the maximum way for the One who deserved my very best, the One who had captivated my heart?* I began to dream about what it would mean to give myself completely to His plan.

During my junior year in college, I sensed the Lord calling me to work with youth. I always had a love and passion for what God could do with them, molding and shaping young lives dedicated to His purpose. I also believed that only lives radically changed by Christ could change our nation and world. I felt so confused—so many opportunities before me.

I wanted God to use me to help change the world. I had mailed a letter off to every mission organization I could think of, asking God to show me where I should go— Africa, China, wherever. I was on my knees when a still, small voice reminded me of another passage in Jeremiah:

"For I know the plans that I have for you," declares the Lord, "plans for welfare and not for calamity to give you a future and a hope. Then you will call upon Me and come and pray to Me, and I will listen to you" (Jeremiah 29:11,12).

It was as if the Holy Spirit said, *I've got it all figured out; I've been leading you along, Nancy. Your love for youth, your discipleship training, your gift for evangelism; I have prepared you for such a time as this. Now take the next step.* I eventually applied for the staff of Campus Crusade for Christ. As I took that next step, God led me to many more steps down the road. It has been quite an adventure, and it's not over yet. I'd like to say I've only just begun.

Is Jesus Christ calling you? In Daniel 11:32 we are reminded, "the people who know their God will display strength and take action." As we learn more of His love and present our lives to the Lord daily, He will guide us into His perfect will. Will we take action, and respond to what He shows us? My prayer is that you will consider what it means to be Chosen With a Mission, and that you will have the courage to respond. I leave you with another poem I wrote, specifically with this moment in mind:

Chosen With a Mission

Can it really be?
One as weak as me?
Chosen by the King—
Quite an awesome thing.
I belong to His Son,
All the work's been done.

Before the world began
And God created man,
He had me in His heart;
That's a radical start!
I'm adopted as His child.
Wouldn't you say, it's wild?
Oh, this gift, this grace
Compels me to run His race.
For I've been set free
To fulfill my destiny;
Marked with His spirit's seal,
This is a done deal.
Called to be His bride,
United at His side;
Jesus, my passion and desire,
Ignite in me Your holy fire
To let my generation know;
Your message of hope I'll show
'Til the whole world sings,
"Glory to the King of kings."
I am chosen with a mission;
It is my King's commission.

—May 25, 1998

Nancy

My Grateful Appreciation

I'm in awe of the Lord's marvelous goodness in bringing this book about! My heart is filled with gratitude for my life-long adventure with Him and the friends who have been with me throughout the journey.

It would be impossible to acknowledge all of those who have inspired and encouraged me during the years of writing this book. I pray that those whom I do not mention will know of my gratitude. Special thanks to:

Those who encouraged me to write this book . . .

🕉 My former pastor, Gene French, and his wife, Shirley, who were the first ones to believe in this project and help me get started.

🕉 Chuck Klein, national director of Student Venture and my associate in ministry, whose expertise and godly counsel helped guide me forward.

🕉 Gioia and Noreen, my missionary sisters in Cambodia, whose faith propelled me.

🕉 Bill and Vonette Bright, co-founders of Campus Crusade for Christ, whose vision and words of encouragement motivated me to finish what God began seven years ago.

Those who provided special places for me to write . . .

🕭 Josh and Dottie McDowell who invited me to use their lovely cabin in Julian, complete with flowers and all!

🕭 The Evangelical Sisters of Mary at Canaan in the Desert in Phoenix and in Darmstadt, Germany, who graciously welcomed and ministered to me.

🕭 Ginger, Rainey, and Jeannine who often opened "God's Place" and their hearts to me.

🕭 Bob & Nadine Gaiser who blessed me with the use of their condominium in St. Petersburg, Florida.

Those who prayed . . .

🕭 Marian Drops, my kindred spirit in the Lord.

🕭 Pearl and Sandy who loved and cheered me on with God's promises.

🕭 Pastor Bill Whitemore, my 96-year-old spiritual mentor.

🕭 Cleona Scope, my precious Trinidadian friend.

🕭 Ben Jennings, who supported me when I needed it the most!

🕭 Don and Molly Lawton, who were always there to lift me up.

🕭 Laurie Killingsworth, my "Passionate Heart" partner.

. . . and too many others to mention.

Those teammates who helped "make it happen!"

🕭 Carol Hill, my former secretary, who provided much valuable editing.

🕭 Kathy Corpus, whose servant heart blessed me as she sacrificially worked to meet deadlines. (Kathy, you're a treasure!)

🕭 Dan, Ken, Cheryl, Stacey, and Gayle-Anne who graciously helped at critical times. (You guys mean a lot!)

🕭 Paul Roberts, an expert editor. (Thanks for getting sucked in . . .

I couldn't have done it without you.)

🌸 Sally Brown, the creative and gifted woman who designed the cover and layout of the book. (Sally, you are a delight to work with! Thanks for giving your all!)

🌸 Erik Segalini, my skillful and gracious editor, who patiently helped me articulate what God put in my heart. (Erik, we've finally arrived! I can't begin to express the joy and privilege it's been to work with you. May you reap rich rewards for the hours you've invested. I'm glad God chose you to be my editor!)

🌸 Emma and Gordon Korell, who sold four of "the Lord's cattle on a thousand hills" to help distribute my book.

Those who have lived the adventure with me . . .

🌸 My Student Venture and Campus Crusade family who walked with me in the adventure and inspired me to "Go for it!"

🌸 My devoted ministry partners, without whom I could not faithfully complete the mission He has called me to.

🌸 My special "long term" friends in "Indy," St. Louis, San Diego, and Springfield.

Those in my precious family . . .

🌸 My extended family who have helped shape my life.

🌸 My four crazy, lovable brothers: Jack, Dan, Keith, Mark (Pal) and their wives. (You guys have been the biggest blessing in my life!)

🌸 My sister and dearest friend Karen. (I love you and your family with all my heart!)

🌸 Mom and Dad, a treasure from my Heavenly Father. (Thanks for pouring into my life and enabling me to embrace life as an adventure!)

Resources

WHO AM I?

I am accepted in Christ.

John 1:12	I am God's child.
John 15:15	I am Christ's friend.
Rom. 5:1	I have been justified.
1 Cor. 6:17	I am united with the Lord, and I am one spirit with Him.
1 Cor. 6:19,20	I have been bought with a price. I belong to God.
1 Cor. 12:27	I am a member of Christ's body.
Eph. 1:1	I am a saint.
Eph. 1:5	I have been adopted as God's child.
Eph. 2:18	I have direct access to God through the Holy Spirit.
Col. 1:14	I have been redeemed and forgiven of all my sins.
Col. 2:10	I am complete in Christ.

I am secure in Christ.

Rom. 8:1,2	I am free forever from condemnation.
Rom. 8:28	I am assured that all things work together for good.
Rom. 8:31-34	I am free from any condemning charges against me.
Rom. 8: 35-39	I cannot be separated from the love of God.
2 Cor. 1:21,22	I have been established, anointed, and sealed by God.
Col. 3:3	I am hidden with Christ in God.

Phil. 3:20	I am a citizen of heaven.
2 Tim 1:7	I have not been given a spirit of fear but of power, love, and sound mind.
Heb. 4:16	I can find grace and mercy in time of need.
1 John 5:18	I am born of God, and the evil one cannot touch me.

I am significant in Christ.

Matt. 5:13,14	I am the salt and light of the earth.
John 15:1,5	I am the branch of the true vine, a channel of His life.
John 15:16	I have been chosen and appointed to bear fruit.
Acts 1:8	I am a personal witness of Christ's.
1 Cor. 3:16	I am God's temple.
2 Cor. 5:17-20	I am a minister of reconciliation for God.
2 Cor. 6:1	I am God's co-worker (I Cor. 3:9)
Eph. 2:6	I am seated with Christ in the heavenly realm.
Eph. 2:10	I am God's workmanship.
Eph. 3:12	I may approach God with freedom and confidence.
Phil. 4:13	I can do all things through Christ who strengthens me.

(Taken from *Living Free in Christ* by Dr. Neil Anderson ©1993, Regal Books)

Active in the Mission

Nancy is associate national director for Student Venture, the high school outreach of Campus Crusade for Christ. In active partnership with local churches and other youth organizations, Student Venture seeks to communicate the love of Christ to every student on every campus in America. This ministry of evangelism and discipleship involves tens of thousands of students and more than 900 full-time staff, volunteers and VITAL LINC affiliates across the U.S.A. and around the world. Many strategies and tools are involved in this effort. Here are two great opportunities that Nancy recommends for youth and their leaders.

Something's Happening Prayer Force

An exciting network of people have committed to seek God for spiritual awakening and revival at their campus and in their community. Hear action reports from around the country, learn tips to strengthen your prayer life, keep informed about the latest prayer gatherings and opportunities, and share your prayer request with the entire Prayer Force—all by connecting to our web site at www.prayerforce.com

Student Venture International Projects

During the past 10 years Student Venture has conducted more than 70 short-term mission projects in the spring and summer. You and your youth group will pack your bags for an adventure as God's messengers to the whole world. For destinations and information call 1.800.699.4678 and ask for the international projects coordinator or write to:

Student Venture International Projects
100 Sunport Lane, Department 3200
Orlando, FL 32809

190

Equipped for the Mission

These additional resources from Nancy will help you in your walk with God. They make a great gift or an easy tool to use in a small group or Sunday school class.

Book Orders

Share your excitement for *Chosen With a Mission* by ordering more copies today. Books are $9.95 each, or buy 10 or more for only $7.95 each. Call 1.800.729.4351.

Speaking Engagements

Capture Nancy's enthusiasm and message in person. Nancy is available to speak at:

- your outreach, conference or retreat
- a Passionate Hearts retreat for women of all ages desiring intimacy with God

For more information or to make arrangements, contact Nancy's assistant at 1.800.699.4678.

Audio Tapes

Hear Nancy's motivating messages on several interesting topics (see next page). Tapes are $3.95 each, or $3 each for quantities of 10 or more of the same topic. Call 1.800.729.4351.

Additional Resources

Call Integrated Resources for other Student Venture materials to help you reach your world: 1.800.729.4351.

Current Titles
(available on audio)

The King's Commission: Respond to God's challenge to be a world-changer and significantly influence your generation.

Secure With Your Singleness: Saying "yes" to the will of God can involve embracing His gift of singleness. Nancy shares her personal experience and God's perspective on the topic.

How to Be Filled With the Spirit: Learn how to experience a dynamic relationship with God through the Holy Spirit's power.

Reaching the Next Generation: A challenging look at how to be women who can influence our generation.

Prayer Is Not an Option: Learn how to tap into the King's power to make a difference in your personal prayer life.

Winning and Discipling Youth to Run God's Race: A vision-packed message filled with "how to's" for developing a ministry to youth.

In Search of the Ideal: Overcome the struggle with comparison, performance, and insecurity as Nancy explains how to replace wrong beliefs with solid truths. Nancy shares her own journey in overcoming an eating disorder.

Journey to the Heart of God: Discover timeless truths about the Father's favor, Jesus' victory and the Holy Spirit's work in your life.

For updated materials and new additions call 1.800.729.4351.

Mail Orders

Order Instructions

Order form is on the back of this page.
Make a photocopy for yourself and mail or call in your order.

Mail to: Integrated Resources
4307 East Third Street
Bloominton, IN 47401
Call: 1.800.729.4351

Allow 2 to 3 weeks for mailed orders.

Prices and Availability: Some prices subject to change. Call to find out the current prices and information about new products. Some products may be discontinued or backordered for reasons beyond our control.

Shipping Time: Most orders leave our office within 24 to 48 hours after receipt of payment.

Method of Payment

❑ Check or Money Order ❑ VISA ❑ MasterCard ❑ Discover
Make all checks payable to: **Integrated Resources**

If payment is to be made with CREDIT CARD, complete boxes below.

_____

CREDIT CARD NUMBER AND EXPIRATION DATE

X_____

SIGNATURE OF CARD HOLDER

ORDER FORM

Books are $9.95 each or buy 10 or more for only $7.95 each.

Tapes are $3.95 each or $3 each for quantities of 10 or more of the same topic or the eight tape set for $20.

Items	Unit Price	Qty.	Total Cost
Books			
1. Chosen With a Mission			
Audio Tapes			
1. The King's Commission			
2. Secure With Your Singleness			
3. How to Be Filled with the Spirit			
4. Reaching the Next Generation			
5. Prayer Is Not an Option			
6. Winning and Discipling Youth...			
7. In Search of the Ideal			
8. Journey to the Heart of God			
TOTAL of all items ordered Used to calculate shipping and handling			
ADD Sales tax:____% of total (Use your Local State Tax Rate)			
ADD Shipping and Handling (see chart below)			
GRAND TOTAL ENCLOSED			

Merchandise Total   Shipping and Handling
$10 or less $3.50
$10.01 to $25.00 .... $5.00
$25.01 to $50.00 .... $6.00
$50.01 to $100.00 .... 9% of the product total
$100.00 or greater .... 7% of product total